$\mathcal{S}$AINTS

Saints

THE CHOSEN FEW

MANUELA DUNN-MASCETTI

BALLANTINE BOOKS · NEW YORK

Library of Congress Catalog Card Number: 94-94177
ISBN: 0-345-38382-6

Produced by Labyrinth Publishing (UK) Ltd.
Design and typesetting by DW Design, London
Manufactured in Italy
First Edition: November 1994

10 9 8 7 6 5 4 3 2 1

CONTENTS

King Richard II being presented to the Virgin and Child by his patron saints: Saint
John the Baptist, Saint Edward the Confessor (with a ring), and Saint Edmund,
King and Martyr. The Wilton Diptych (c. 1395) National Gallery, London.

PART ONE

DEFINING SAINTHOOD

PART ONE

DEFINING SAINTHOOD

CHAPTER ONE
THE OTHERWORLDLY VIRTUES OF SAINTS

"They lost their tempers, got hungry, scolded God, were egotistical or testy or impatient in their turns, made mistakes and regretted them. Still they went on doggedly blundering toward Heaven. And they won sanctity partly by willing to be saints, not only because they encountered no temptation to be less."

(Phyllis McGinley)

If we were asked the question "What is a saint?" and we had had no previous experience of an encounter with such a person, how would we satisfy the enquirer's curiosity? Would we point to models of piety and virtue, concepts that most of us regard as belonging to an age gone by? Would we answer by saying that saints are mostly historical figures considered holy by one religion or another? Or would we, in fact, have to admit that we really don't know the answer?

Perhaps our ignorance can be excused by the fact that it mirrors a certain cultural numbness of our age, an age that seems to be uncomfortable with talk of religious power, or how this power is manifested in individuals. The whole dilemma hints at our disenchantment in matters of both religion and religious individuals – our pantheon of saints may seem to be narrow, decrepit, old, and made up of notions that no longer apply to the fast and furious pace of modern life. And yet, more and more people are discovering a gap within themselves which cannot be filled by material acquisitions, or even by the values we were brought up to believe would give us eternal satisfaction.

As one way of curing this emptiness, it seems that more and more people are beginning to turn towards paradigms of humanity which convey an image of "wholeness" and "inner peace." Thus, exceptional individuals like the Dalai Lama, Mother Teresa, or Ram Dass, draw large crowds wherever they appear.

Page 9: *His Holiness the Dalai Lama visiting Sarnath.* Below: *Large crowds gather to hear the message of the Dalai Lama.* Opposite: *Gandhi, a saint of the people, stands on the step at 10 Downing Street, London, residence of the British Prime Minister. Both the Dalai Lama and Gandhi incarnate the modern paradigm of spirituality.*

There is an increasing revival of interest in messages which question the ethical codes that bind society and our individual lives. The need for saints – for religious individuals who point us towards the correct path for inner and outer survival – is growing, and the call for help reverberates throughout the world.

Thus the search to know what a saint is and what function this person has within the community represents a contemporary plea for guidance, and it touches the whole of humanity across the religious spectrum. If we look to the past for solutions to the religious stagnation which characterizes our modern age, we find that saints were once seen as the impregnators of the world, vivifiers, and animators of potentialities within us that would lie dormant had they not been awakened by the saintly presence. The saints, as we shall see in this book, are spiritual fires that kindle our hearts and souls, creating new fires. Saints took the first step towards higher realities and assumed the ensuing risks. To reach our own higher potentialities, we must honor that courage by listening to their stories and allowing ourselves to be inspired by them.

WHAT IS A SAINT?

Mankind, it has been said, is incurably religious, captive to an inescapable predicament that is integral to the soul. Any individual, therefore, who is manifestly connected to sacred reality – in the form of God, gods and goddesses, spiritual powers, or mythical realms – has always been held in veneration by the people. It is as if the saintly figure is a loving reminder that our ultimate aspirations, however impossible they may seem, are in fact achievable. Like us, they are human beings – but unlike us they are human incarnations of divine power.

Saints have always been mysterious, for they are wholly human and yet they have privileged contact with the supernatural. They perform miracles, receive visions, and are strangely enamored of the spirit. In their "holiness" they leave the rest of humanity wondering. Indeed, the very notion of sainthood suggests that it is a quality pertaining only to certain individuals, "the chosen few," irrespective of their religion.

If we engage in a cross-cultural examination of what a saint is, we plunge deeply into the richness and variety of the religious traditions that have given birth to so many exceptional individuals. We find saints everywhere and in all times. Representing the ripe fruits of religion, they incarnate the divine and bring its love, goodness, and spiritual climate down to earth for all of us to enjoy. This cross-cultural examination also helps us to fill the gaps where there is a vacuum in our own religious traditions. If saints are living embodiments of what we consider to be religiousness, then it logically follows that what makes one a saint varies from religion to religion. However, if saints appear everywhere, then there must be universal traits that unify them and make them easily recognizable to all, regardless of any specific religious ideology.

So what are the qualities held in common by the saintly? First, the saint is a source of power. Indeed the saint exudes power, affecting both people and the processes of nature. Hindu saints, for example, are believed to be focal points of "spiritual force-fields,"

in the sense that they literally alter the quality of the energy that surrounds them. They generate and are surrounded by a "Buddha-field" which can profoundly affect those who come in contact with it, and provoke an immediate and personal experience of meditation in those who are receptive.

This quality of power has been recognized as "holy" or "supernatural" by human beings for as long as we have existed on earth. It can be recognized in the term "mana," used by Polynesians and Melanesians to describe that which affects and transforms both people and nature. It finds expression in the languages of the Native American tribes also, as the "orenda" of the Iroquois, "wakan" of the Dakotas, and "manitou" of the Algonquin. The power of the saint is the power of nature – and of the divinity inherent in that nature – personified.

But the saint is not simply one who wields divine power. It is the function of saints which is important to us and explains why the need for saints has never died. The world's religions promote articles of faith and codes of conduct that are intended to put us on the right path towards spiritual fulfillment; however, we don't learn by obeying precepts, "oughts" and "shoulds," alone. Something far more inspiring is needed to ring a bell within our spirits, something –

or better, someone – we can all identify with and love. Really, what we want to hear are not religious and moral codes but stories; not precepts but personalities; not lectures but lives. It is the function of the saints to fulfill this human desire – this is where their true power lies.

What do saints do for us? Why is the phenomenon of sainthood so widespread throughout all history and in almost all religious traditions? The Second Vatican Council on the phenomenon of sainthood gives us some clues:

"Let the faithful be taught, therefore, that the authentic cult of the saints consists not so much in the multiplying of external acts, but rather in the intensity of our active love. By such love, for our own greater good and that of the Church, we seek from the saints example in their way of life, fellowship in their communion, and aid in their intercession."

Example, fellowship, and aid are easily defined universal traits that unite the saints in all religious traditions. These represent three bridges of communication between holy beings and humanity, within which their gifts become available to us, and whereby we are healed and transformed by the divine force they command.

Right: *A popular religious image of Saint Francis of Assisi.* Opposite: *An illuminated manuscript portraying six Franciscan monks arriving in Flanders. Saint Francis remains a powerful example of godliness for religious orders and laity alike.*

THE SAINT AS EXAMPLE

Saints can be examples of someone (God), or of something (godliness). Often, of course, they are both – and sometimes, one must admit, they appear to be neither! Many disciples and entire religious communities follow examples set by particular saints (which is why we commonly call disciples "followers"). Franciscan monks, for instance, take vows of chastity, fraternity, and poverty when joining the order – these were virtues that Saint Francis himself represented and encouraged among his followers. These same virtues were known from the Christian scriptures as some of the qualities of Jesus, and thus Saint Francis became eligible for sainthood because he reflected aspects of the Son of God. Franciscan monks follow the example of Francis with the purpose of developing these same virtues.

However, to become a saint requires more than just a talent for imitation. The saintly individual must exude the virtues from the very soul, without manifesting any effort to do so – as though he or she is directly endowed with this gift by God. As Francis De Sales, a French saint, stated, "Sanctity does not consist in being odd, but it does consist in being rare." The spiritual virtues promoted by religious scriptures may seem utterly unachievable by ordinary human beings. However, when these virtues are displayed by the saints, they take on flesh and blood. Because the saints are human like us, we can measure ourselves against them. Their goodness and perfection can be seen as our own potential for goodness and perfection. In writings related to the Buddha's disciples, for instance, we find highlights on Ananda's compassion, Sariputta's wisdom, or Moggallana's magical powers. Their stories become instruments of teaching, for when holiness is seen within a human setting it becomes more accessible to us.

The saint, therefore, is someone from whom others can learn patterns of life that no principle or spiritual and moral code can give. Another example of this is found in the early Christian saints of the late Roman Empire – the point in history at which the Christian cult of the saints was generated. Here we meet saints whose behavior was such that they literally became "representations of Christ" rather than mere transmitters of the "image of God." These men and women carried Christ with such totality as to "re-present" for their followers the

light and force that had characterized Jesus himself; in other words, they became Christ for those who had not known him.

These early Christian saints, and others in different religions, showed a way through to a higher level of existence so coherently and with such passion that in contrast to ordinary life, ridden as it was with doubt and fears, they seemed able to generate their own light. The language of luminosity permeates stories about their lives. Meetings with them are described in terms of "flashes of light," "shining visions," and breakthroughs from darkness to light (which, interestingly, is the literal translation of the Hindi word "guru"). Jewish accounts of the enigmatic teachers known as "tsaddiqqim" tell of a similar palpable glow, and they are described in terms that suggest they have left the human realm altogether and appear to be channels for the divine.

This luminous, otherworldly quality is also one of the staple characteristics of Hindu saints, and devotees travel great distances to obtain the "sight" ("darsan" in Hindi) of those they venerate. For these saints, as for those in most of the Eastern traditions, the journey from unknowing humanity to holiness is a process of "becoming enlightened" – either suddenly in one huge thunderbolt from above, or gradually upon a path that may last several lifetimes.

It is always a matter of wonder and celebration that the extraordinary light of the saints manages to touch the world; this may well be one of the fundamental miracles performed by saints.

The Annunciation to Saint Anne, by Giotto, in the Cappella degli Scrovegni, Padua.

THE SAINTLY RING OF FELLOWSHIP

The second trait common to all holy individuals across the religious spectrum is the sense of fellowship they provide for ordinary human beings who embark upon the spiritual path. In their intimate and direct contact with the faithful, they span the gap between the known and the unknown. They seem to be entirely at ease with the densely mysterious forces that govern life, affirming the essentially sacred character of these forces. As a consequence they have been made, over the centuries, patrons and protectors of churches, temples, towns, natural groves, or other sacred places where people gather, both to affirm their individual aspirations to the divine and to celebrate the companionship of fellow travelers on the sacred journey.

Saints come in flocks to puzzle us, and we can argue that one of their functions is to provide an image of a divine society, "the chosen few." In this sense, the community of saints in any religion serves as a family that nurtures and oversees the spiritual progress of the individual. We may draw great comfort from the fact that there is someone available other than God or a priest, and consequently there is an urge to venerate these exemplary guardian figures.

There is a notion in Judaism, for instance, that there exists a core elite of "righteous ones" (the tsaddiqim) who link the generations in a moral bond extending far into the past. In Islamic thought, the saints are seen as a divine community who form an invisible hierarchy in the world. Allah is believed to

Saint Bernard's ring, kept as a relic in his sanctuary in the Swiss Alps.

Below: *An illuminated page from a manuscript by Hildegard of Bingen, a medieval German mystic, representing the cosmic communion of saints.*
Opposite: *Srila Prabhupada, Founder–Acarya of the International Society for Krishna Conciousness.*

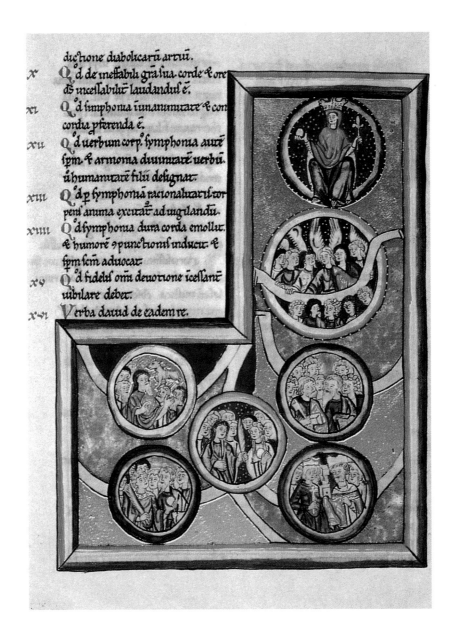

have distributed them on a regular basis to different generations and communities to prepare the people for the coming of his prophet Mohammed. The Christians have long referred to this fellowship as "communio sanctorum," which effectively oversees the doings of human beings.

This group of witnesses may be superior to man in spiritual accomplishments, but they also share lives that are intertwined with ours. Hearing their individual stories, we feel comforted that a saint has known the tribulations of being human, and that in many cases it is exactly those tribulations that have brought him or her to a higher realm. Their very presence among us gives deeper meaning to our actions, and shows us that our own expansion and development need not be restricted either by circumstances of birth or limitations of a given social order. By remaining a society apart, a class of their own, the saints offer an alternative path and goal.

The presence of the saint, or the example of his or her spiritual flowering from the "mud" of ordinary life, is also a powerful point of attraction and tends to center the spiritual seeker upon the path. We might wonder, along with Saint Augustine, that men go abroad to marvel at the heights of mountains, at the huge waves of the sea, at the long courses of the rivers, at the circular motion of the stars and planets, and yet they pass by themselves without a second glance. To meet a saint, to travel upon his or her path for a while, returns us to ourselves.

Below: *A statue of the Virgin Mary stands in a simple shrine at Saint Non's Well, in Dyfed, Wales.* Opposite: *The portrait of Saint Anthony of Padua in the basilica dedicated to him.*

Below: *An assembly of Muslim saints.* Opposite: *A Buddhist master addressing his followers.*

THE SAINT PROVIDES AID

Saints are possessed of divine power; they embody it, manifest it, and demonstrate divine qualities for a wider public. Central to the saint's power is the gift to effect changes in the lives of others. They do not, however, ultimately own the force they command. The saints are in effect channels for the divine power to be made manifest on earth. Only devotion to a higher divinity allows them access to their powers; thus, they both attend to devotees and are themselves devotees to a higher God. This symmetry of roles allows them to mediate between the seen and unseen realms.

Traditionally, there are several ways in which we can gain access to saintly power: prayer, petition, and contact with a talisman or relic left behind. Relics of the saints are said to provide luminous insight into human affairs and, at the same time, they offer a sense of reassurance to devotees as solid evidence of divine origin. Should a woman have trouble in conceiving, for example, she can appeal to Saint Mary. Should she wish to aid herself in love, then she might light a candle to Saint Anthony of Padua. She is in effect appealing to people with more power than her own to bring fulfillment to her desires.

Part of the popular faith in sainthood is related to how much power saints can generate to effect change in people's lives. Their power is sometimes sought to influence relatively mundane desires. Sathya Sai Baba, an Indian "saint," for example, is acclaimed for producing expensive jewelry and watches for his devotees. Others have been known to help win lotteries. Still others assist and oversee travels or heal sickness. Generally, the goal of saintly aid is to help the disciple toward a greater sense of well-being, as well as to increase his sense of morality, encouraging him further along the spiritual path.

Left: *A monk of the Order of Saint Bernard stands in front of a statue of Our Blessed Lady.*

Saintly virtue is never just ordinary virtue in perfected form. Saints contravene pious expectations as much as they fulfill them; they transform dogmatic morality into a personal, and thus more genuine, accessible, and contagious interpretation. They give us the hope that we might become saintly just by accepting the way we are, that our basic human characteristics may also be touched by God. It might even appear that saints really enjoy manifesting their sainthood in the most peculiar and wonderful ways.

As the eleventh-century saint Bernard of Clairvaux said: "What else do worldlings think we are doing but playing about when we flee what they most desire on earth, and what they flee, we desire? We are like jesters and tumblers who, with heads down and feet in the air draw all eyes to themselves. ... Ours is a joyous game, decent, grave, and admirable, delighting the gaze of those who watch from heaven."

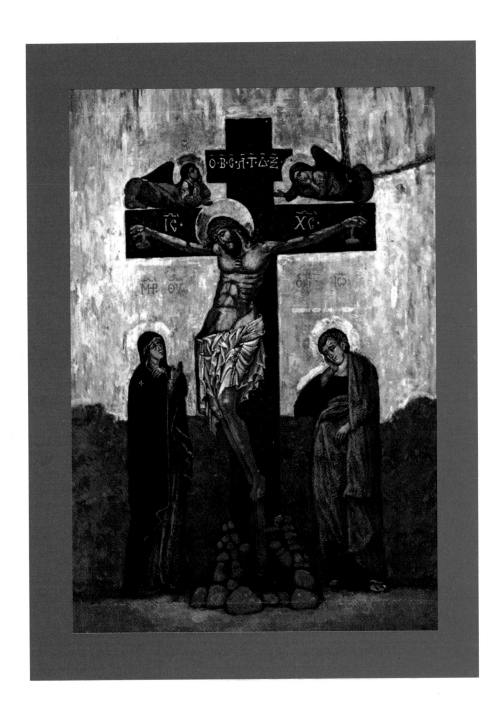

CHAPTER TWO

SAINTHOOD IN THE CHRISTIAN TRADITION

Christianity would be unthinkable without sinners, unlivable without saints. The Acts of the Apostles provide the core models of Christian behavior, experience, and identity. As long as Christianity has existed it has venerated the holy men and women who lived, died, were martyred, had visions, performed miracles, instituted new religious orders, heroically confessed their faith under the greatest duress, imitated, and existed exclusively for Christ. As Saint Paul declared, "I live; yet not I, but Christ liveth in me."

The official Canon of the Catholic Church celebrates a different saint each day of the year. In addition to these there are several hundred more saints, many of whom are largely forgotten, and further hundreds of would-be saints waiting to be included in this list of the spiritually privileged. In order to accommodate them all – the saints mentioned in the official Canon and the ones that the Church might have overlooked or failed to proclaim as such – there is a celebration on the first day of November, appropriately named "All Saints' Day." In the Roman Catholic countries almost every village and town has a patron saint. It would be impossible to count the shrines and the official and unofficial festivities dedicated to Christian saints, let alone try and estimate the number of devotees who pray every day to receive the grace and be granted the favors of a particular holy being.

Opposite: *The persecution that had brought Jesus to die on the cross was to become the fate of every new Christian – prejudice, oppression, and martyrdom.* Above: *Kilmalkedar, County Kerry, Ireland, is a pilgrimage site dedicated to the Blessed Virgin Mary, the most venerated of Christian saints.*

Below: *To believe is, in Christian terms, to suffer, and faith calls for sacrifice. This image of the suffering Christ is from an illuminated manuscript by the medieval mystic Hildegard. Opposite: The baptism of Jesus by John the Baptist, by the Italian painters Lorenzo and Jacopo Salimbeni. Redemption from sin starts with baptism shortly after birth.*

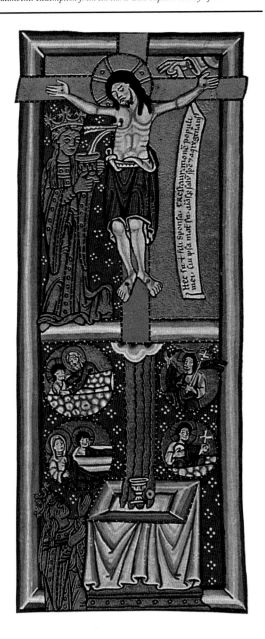

The English word "saint" is derived from the Latin "sanctus", which is an equivalent of the Greek "hagios" and of the Hebrew "qadosh" – three words used in ancient times to designate, respectively, God, people (emperors, deceased relatives, and others), and things. When the terms were applied to people and things they connoted solemnity and consecration – that is, the object was in some way set apart for a sacred purpose or ritual, "made holy to God." The words did not originally carry the moral connotations that later became associated with them within the framework of Christianity.

The development of sainthood in the Christian tradition is a history made by individuals, with special emphasis upon their extraordinary roles. The religion's support of the doctrine of the soul – whereby one stands alone before God on the day of judgment, attains salvation as an individual, and goes on to enjoy personal survival after death – is a good example of this. Other indications of this emphasis are found in the unique role ascribed to Jesus Christ as founder of the religion, the perennial fascination for Christians of their spiritual and ecclesiastical leaders, and the cult of personality which is so markedly underscored in the development of the Christian notion of sainthood. Of all the major religions –Christianity, Islam, Buddhism, Hinduism, and Judaism – Christianity seems to have placed the most weight on the freedom, potential, and responsibility of the individual. Thus, the veneration of the saints orbits around historical people, "the chosen few," who have been touched by God.

The cult of sainthood has been a powerful movement in Christianity, so powerful in fact that at one point it threatened to rival the worship of God and thereby resemble the idolatrous, polytheistic veneration of the ancient pagan religions that Christianity had fought to substitute. This was perhaps the main concern behind the drive of the Church to establish a proper way to worship saints ("doulia"), sharply distinct from the worship owed to Christ ("latria"), and for the gradual and effectual bureaucratization of the process of "making" saints.

The Christian faith is focused on a crucified man and, one might say, as a logical consequence the history of Christian sainthood is a long path strewn with thorns and the suffering of individuals bearing the cross in the name of their belief. The apostles were warned by Christ himself that the choice they had made exposed them to death, and that this would always be the case. To believe is, in Christian terms, to suffer, and faith calls for sacrifice. In keeping to the gospel that made its members endure death rather than renounce the faith, Christians were in the beginning persecuted and later they inflicted persecution on others. The history of sainthood in the Christian tradition bears witness to this fatal combination in countless ways.

THE MARTYRS

The word "cult" has nowadays gained negative connotations in the popular mind, and is commonly used to describe a pseudo-religious movement which exists on the fringes of organized religious understanding. Modern cults are small, flickering flames of beliefs that might be extinguished by the gust of a more established dogma. We need to remind ourselves that Christianity in its beginning was a cult, with all the modern connotations of the word, developing in the midst of Judaism and the powerful Greco-Roman pantheon, and its flame could have been blown out at any time.

The tiny Christian sect spread after the resurrection of Jesus, proclaiming a teaching which rang bells until then unheard: God, made man, was born, lived, died,

Above: *Saint Clether Well Chapel, in Cornwall, England. Water flows through this chapel into an outer channel. Relics of the saint were kept by the water in order to maintain their healing power.* Right: *The martyrdom of Saints Cosmas and Demian. The early martyrs found death a direct route to sainthood, for to die for Christ and like Christ was then, and still is, the strongest proof of holiness.*

and rose again for the salvation of mankind. These Christians were bringing news, in the words of Saint Paul, of an "unknown God." The Greco-Roman pagans could accept the idea of the incarnation of God into man, for their own pantheon of gods and goddesses frequently adopted human form for escapades in the mortal world. The same idea, however, offended the Jews, who held very strong beliefs about divine transcendence.

Had the early Christians merely declared that Christ survived death, Christianity would perhaps never have achieved any success, for such a concept was similar to the superhuman powers held by Greco-Roman heroes. What troubled Rome was the strange zeal which inflamed this sect of newly converted Jews. There existed no strong tradition of proselytizing in Judaism, yet the Christians, whose cult was born out of Judaism, sent out traveling missionaries to repeat Jesus' sermons from village to village. They baptized people en masse, promised eternal life after death, and claimed that their "lord" was the one and only true king. Thus they directly challenged both the religious authority of the Jews and the divine right of the Roman emperor to be recognized as the ultimate "lord." Both were unforgivable insults. When confronted with the crime, the Christians not only

The crypt beneath Ripon cathedral, Yorkshire, containing the relics of Saint Wilfred, one of the first British saints.

refused to repent, but were ready to die in order to defend their faith, so that laws and weapons used against them were rendered completely powerless.

Christianity competed with the established religious orders not for a higher sense of morality, which would have caused less havoc and drawn a less bloody history, but for eternal life, and as a new religion it subverted the established religious and political order – ultimately posing a political problem. Thus, early Christians were beheaded, sent to the stake, and thrown to the wild beasts. The predicament that had brought Jesus to die on the cross was to become the predicament of every new Christian.

The early martyrs welcomed death because it was a direct route to eternal life; just as Jesus had obeyed the Father until death, so the good Christian would die not only for Christ, but also like Christ. In fact, even today, martyrdom remains the surest path to official canonization and more martyrs have been proclaimed holy than any other category of saint. To die as a Christian in defense of the faith was to be reborn in the fullness of life everlasting, and to be blessed by God the Father himself. Emperor Julian the Apostate accused the Christians by stating: "You keep adding many corpses newly dead to the corpse [Christ] of long ago. You have filled the whole world with tombs and sepulchers."

This passion for death, both as the symbol of the cult and as the ultimate obstacle to Rome's ability to force Christians to conform to the laws, inflamed the Romans even further. Persecution increased, and as a consequence Mass was held in secret locations in the dead of night. To become a Christian in this era almost invariably meant embracing the risk of torture and martyrdom.

The Romans were trying to punish the new sect, to dissuade the new converts from maintaining their faith, and to divert popular attention from the new religion. Their attempt to show that, by exposing themselves to torture and death, the Christians were being deprived of the religion they held so dear, failed completely.

The most common form of punishment was to send the victims to be eaten alive by the wild beasts of the circus. This had long been a popular form of entertainment in Roman times. Not only did it amuse the crowds, but the blood shed during the games was purported to have regenerative power among the mighty Roman nobles. They could thank the gods for never having been slaves to barbarians, and thus symbolically renew their conquest of the Empire. The gladiators, who engaged in hand-to-hand combat and fought against the beasts, were recruited from barbarian slaves caught in battle, and the excitement of the games was derived from the sight of these bloody combats.

However, when the Christians came along, ready to be punished for their religion, the crowds saw

Above left: The Colosseum in Rome, where the early Christians were thrown to the wild beasts. Above: The martyrdom of Saint Ignatius, bishop of Antioch in Syria. He was thrown to the beasts in Rome c.107 CE.

elderly men, women, and children thrown into the ring with neither armor nor weapons with which to defend themselves. The spectacle was made even more poignant by the fact that the newcomers not only failed to fight but allowed themselves to be savaged without resisting, so eager were they to enter the promised bliss of the afterlife. Ignatius of Antioch, an early martyr, wrote to the Christians of Rome:

"May I benefit from the wild beasts prepared for me, and I pray that they will be found prompt with me, whom I shall even entice to devour me promptly — not as with some whom they were too timid to touch; and should they not consent voluntarily, I shall force them."

The martyrs thus soon became the focus of the new cult of Christianity. These spiritual athletes were a living proof of the power of their new God, so visibly at work and in such a dramatic way. The victims were symbolically important for new converts to Christianity, who drew power from the martyrs' strength of faith. Their willingness to die was perceived as miraculous, and these individuals became the new models of conduct. Their extraordinary commitment to the faith renewed the zeal of other adherents of the religion to proclaim its truth. If initially the word saint was applied to the members of the Christian community at large, it was soon reserved exclusively for martyrs. Sainthood and martyrdom became hardly distinguishable.

Following their gruesome deaths, the remains of the saints were carefully transported to the location

The martyrdom and funeral of Saint Ursula, a Christian British princess said to have been killed along with 11,000 virgins by the Huns in Cologne. This painting by Vittore Carpaccio (1460 - c.1526), is in the Accademia in Venice.

THE MARTYRDOM OF SAINT STEPHEN

Saint Stephen was the first Christian to be martyred in Jerusalem where he died in the year 35 CE. He is celebrated on the 26th day of December. Stephen was a Greek-speaking Jew "full of faith and power," who was chosen by the apostles as the first deacon to look after the needs of Greek-speaking widows among the Christians in Jerusalem. He was also a zealous preacher and performed many miracles and wonders. These activities, however, caused him to be denounced to the Jewish council as a blasphemer. When he was brought before the council, he addressed it at length, telling the history of Israel, and ending his speech by accusing his hearers of resisting the Holy Spirit just as their forefathers had done. Looking towards the sky, he said, "Behold, I see the heavens opened, and the Son of Man standing at the right hand of God." Thereupon the elders rushed him out of the city and stoned him to death. During his martyrdom, Stephen cried out, "Lord Jesus, receive my spirit. ... Lord, lay not this sin to their charge!" Standing by and approving the execution was a young man from Tarsus, called Saul, who was to become Saint Paul of the gentiles.

Above: *The martyrdom of Saint Stephen.* Opposite left: *The faithful gather in Saint Peter's Square in the Vatican, awaiting the Pope's declaration that a saint must be venerated throughout Catholic churches in the world.* Right: *Base of the shrine of Saint Bertram, a fourteenth-century British saint, in the church at Ilam, Staffordshire. The holes allowed pilgrims to get as close as possible to the heart of the shrine.*

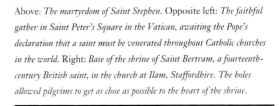

where Mass was celebrated, in the catacombs or other secret tombs. There, the remains were buried and on the anniversary of the death of the saint, a special ceremony was held to venerate the holy being. Thus tomb and altar were joined. With time, the tombs of the saints where the relics were kept became locations of pilgrimage, and eventually churches were built on the sites in order to provide the faithful with an appropriate place of worship. The Basilica of Saint Peter in Rome is a good example of this, originally built over the grave of the apostle. Still today a church is, by definition of the Catholic Church's Code of Canon Law, a holy place housing the tomb containing the relics of a saint.

The remains of the bodies which the martyrs had sacrificed so willingly became, for the surviving communities, holy relics with a special power. Even though it was understood that the spirit of the victim had risen to heaven, it was believed that it was also still present in a special way – in essence – in the bones and in whatever else was left over after the martyrdom, even including the instruments of torture. It was believed that the will to die was derived from a power that came to the martyr directly from God, just as it had come to Jesus on the cross from the Father. And, by magical association, people believed that if they came into contact with the dead body of the saint they too would receive their share. People were known to throw handkerchiefs and other pieces of clothing at the saint's body in the hope that the divine power would be magically entrapped in them. These objects, in turn,

were also highly prized and treasured as wonder-making relics. This practice, started more than a thousand years ago, is still continued today. Devotees still flock to a saint's church and touch the statue, or tomb, or whatever object represents the saint, believing that the contact will guarantee a blessing.

If the blessed power of the saints is present in their holy relics, so their strength of faith was recorded in the stories of their martyrdom. In the early centuries of Christianity, narratives of the saints' passion and death kept the faith alive in the face of constant and cruel persecution. Whenever Christians were martyred a story was written, often in the form of a letter addressed to other Christians. These accounts traveled from community to community, inflaming the religious fervor of the new converts and augmenting the reputation of the saint.

Above: *Reliquary of a bone of Saint Chad in Saint Chad's Cathedral, Birmingham, England. It is believed that a saint's power resides in every part of his or her body, before and after death. Every relic of the saint was therefore revered.* Opposite: *Sainthood in the early Church found expression in extreme ascetism. In time, monasteries were built to protect the hermit monks. The iconostasis, separating the sanctuary from the nave, in Saint Catherine's monastery, Sinai.*

The earliest written account of martyrdom is that of Saint Polycarp, the bishop of Smyrna, who is said to have been a disciple of Saint John and a great teacher. His death, which occurred in 156 CE, was recorded in a letter sent by the Christian community in Smyrna to other Christians across the empire. At the time all the Christians who were arrested were being put to death by the authorities. Their main crime was refusal to sacrifice to the gods, which effectively meant that they did not recognize the absolute sovereignty of the emperor and by implication were indifferent to the well-being of both the nation and mankind. Often, in fact, the new Christians were put to death more to allay the superstitious fears of the masses than because they represented a real threat to the authorities.

The Church of the first centuries can be seen as a long procession of martyrs – old and young, men, women, and children, rich and poor, educated and simple. Since the accounts written about their deaths were intended to glorify the saints as much as to edify the readers, they are laced with legends and accounts of miracles and wonders. Even though they are today deemed historically unreliable, they do give us an insight into the attitudes of both the Church and the faithful towards the saints, and the ways in which sanctity was perceived, imagined, and recorded for posterity.

The persecution of Christian communities unfolded in three different historical stages: the first wave of violence was unleashed with the burning of Rome, which Nero blamed on the Christians.

The Martyrdom of Saint Polycarp

Hearing the rumors of persecutions of Christians, Polycarp was not dismayed, but wished to remain in Smyrna. Friends and disciples convinced him to seek refuge in a small house, on the outskirts of the city. Here he remained with his friends, praying day and night for the salvation of the Christian men and women who were being put to death by the authorities. While praying he fell into a trance for three days, during which he saw his pillow being consumed by fire, a symbol he interpreted as meaning that he would be killed by being burned alive.

As there was an active search for him, it was deemed safest that he move to another house. However, his pursuers broke into his first house and, not finding him there, they seized two young slaves. One of them broke down under torture and led the constables and horsemen to Polycarp's new hiding place. Once again he could have escaped, but this time he refused, saying, "The Lord's will be done."

When he was sure that everyone had arrived, Polycarp came down from the upper floor and talked with them and offered them food and drink. Then he asked the authorities to give him an hour to pray undisturbed. When permission was given, he stood and prayed for a long time, and many of those watching, seeing how old and noble he was, felt great guilt for having attacked him.

When he ended his prayer, Polycarp was brought to the city on a donkey where he was handed over to Herod, the high sheriff, and Herod's father, Nicetes. They tried to persuade him to negate his faith by asking, "What is the harm in saying 'Caesar is Lord,' and offering incense, and so on, and saving your life?" He answered that he did not intend to be advised by them. When Polycarp entered the stadium, a voice was heard by the Christians who surrounded him. The voice seemed to come from heaven and said, "Be strong, Polycarp, and play the man." The proconsul interrogated him, threatened him, and tried to persuade him to negate his faith. Polycarp derided all the proconsul's attempts and reiterated that he was a Christian. When the proconsul threatened that he would have him consumed by fire, Polycarp replied, "You threaten me with a fire that burns for an hour and is speedily quenched; so you know nothing of the fire of the judgment to come and of the eternal punishment which is reserved for the wicked. Why delay? Give your orders."

Finally the proconsul sent his herald to proclaim three times in the middle of the stadium that Polycarp had confessed to being a Christian. A pyre was built, and Polycarp disrobed in preparation for his martyrdom. When the authorities were about to nail him to the cross, he asked that they leave him as he was, for he would remain unflinching at the stake without the safeguard of nails. So they bound him with rope and when he had finished his last prayer, they set the pyre on fire. But a miracle happened—the fire formed an arch like a ship's sail billowing in the wind, and made a wall around the body of Polycarp, which was "in the middle, almost as though it were bread in the oven." A sweet perfume, "like frankincense or some other precious spice," emanated from the body of the saint.

At last, when it became clear that Polycarp's body could not be consumed by fire, an executioner was ordered to stab him with a dagger. As this was done, another miracle occurred: a dove flew out of his wound and also such a great gush of blood that it extinguished the fire. However, Polycarp died from the loss of blood. The authorities burned the body, and the Christians were later able to take away the ashes. The saint is now commemorated on the 26th day of January.

The heart of the first native-born saint of South America – San Roque Gonzales.

Throughout the second century persecution was incoherent and badly organized. In the third century it seemed that the Empire had become more merciful and open to a reconciliation between paganism and the new religion. But everything changed in the year 250 CE when the emperor Decius, alarmed by the fast expansion of the new faith, ordered that all citizens must sacrifice publicly to the gods. For the Christians this decree was equivalent to a death sentence. In every city, watch committees were appointed, sending many Christians to their deaths. After twenty methodical and bloody years, the persecution eventually slackened. But in 303 CE the persecution of Christians broke out with a new violence. The faith was spreading so fast and with such threatening

The Donation of Constantine restored Christians' freedom of worship and returned their confiscated property. By embracing Christianity, the Roman Emperor Constantine effectively made the Empire a Christian state.

political consequences – the only power Christians recognized was that of their own Lord – that the strength of the response seems to have reflected the sheer despair of the authorities at not being able to keep it under control. Four edicts were published with the hope of keeping the Christian thirst for martyrdom and consequent sanctity within controllable boundaries. The first ordered that all instruments of worship – churches, books, and objects – be destroyed. The second ordered the imprisonment of the clergy. The third condemned to death Christians who persisted in their faith. And the fourth obliged all citizens to sacrifice to the gods on pain of death. But the number of Christians did not cease to grow. With the passing of years the laws gradually allowed for an indulgence of the faith, which was after all inevitably taking over. In 313 CE the Edict of Milan, signed by Constantine, the first Christian emperor, officially put an end to the persecutions.

Above: *The Rose window in the transept at Westminster Abbey in London.* Right: *A seal depicting King Edward I, also known as Edward the Confessor.* Opposite: *The Coronation Chair at Westminster Abbey. The Chair was the throne of Edward I. It rests upon the Stone of Scone, which was brought by Edward from Scotland and is believed to be the stone upon which Jacob laid his head, as related in the Old Testament.*

SAINT EDWARD THE CONFESSOR

Edward was born at Islip around the year 1004, the son of Ethelred II, King of the English, and Emma, sister of Duke Richard II of Normandy, where the young Edward lived until he was recalled to England in 1041. He succeeded to the throne in 1042, and a year later he married Edith, daughter of the ambitious and powerful Earl Godwin. Edward's reign was peaceful, for the king was a peace-loving man.

The belief that Edward was a saint grew out of his religious devotion, his generosity to the poor and ill, and the miracles he supposedly performed. He was believed to possess the "divine touch of kings" which cured scrofula, a general description for many diseases of the time. He and his wife Edith were said to be such ascetics that they lived as brother and sister. The marriage was in fact childless.

Edward was buried in the church of the abbey at Westminster, which at the time was but a small monastery that he had had lavishly refurbished. Saint Edward the Confessor is the only English saint whose bodily remains still rest in their medieval shrine. He is celebrated on the 13th day of October.

THE TEMPTATIONS OF SAINT ANTHONY

Anthony was born near Memphis around the year 251 CE. When he was about twenty years of age, he went to live alone near his home in Lower Egypt, spending his time in prayer and study, and keeping himself by manual work which brought enough income for him to survive. He underwent violent temptations, both physical and spiritual, which he successfully overcame, and within a number of years disciples had gathered around him. In 320 CE he moved farther away and made his hermitage in a cave on Mount Kolzim, near the northwest corner of the Red Sea. This was to remain his home until his death.

Saint Anthony is considered to be the founder of monasticism, because he gathered hermits in closely-knit communities. His austerity and asceticism were wholly directed towards the better service of God, and he served as an excellent model for spiritual wisdom. His influence was very great, and extended far throughout Christendom with the effect that he was venerated until well into the Middle Ages. Anthony is celebrated on the 17th day of January.

Opposite: *The Temptations of Saint Anthony, by Hieronymus Bosch, Museo del Prado, Madrid.*

CONFESSORS AND ASCETICS

With Constantine's grant of toleration of Christianity, the faithful were faced with a new era, punctuated by new trials and temptations. Christians were no longer put to death for their beliefs and were, for the first time, free to worship their God. In a sense this posed a problem for sanctity: until now, sainthood had been synonymous with martyrdom, because willingness to die for Christ presupposed divine intervention. Only the power of God could sustain the martyrs until the end, and all the sins committed in life were erased. No greater proof of faith could be asked from a good Christian.

It was one thing to recognize holiness in martyrs, but quite another to recognize it in non-martyrs. Without the trial of death, how was one to judge the strength of a person's faith? A new proof of sanctity was called for, and the early Middle Ages saw a new model of sainthood arise in the guise of the confessors. These men and women literally "confessed" their faith by bearing witness to Christ in life, as the martyrs had done previously in death. Thus, in the following centuries, bishops, nuns, monks, and other members of the clergy were added to the list of martyr saints, for they had lived for and like Christ.

Another model for sainthood arose in the form of asceticism. By the rigors of their discipline, the ascetics purified the spirit in order to erase all trace of sin. Leaving behind town and village, these hermits embraced the solitude of the deserts and other remote locations, and there strove to achieve the same purity of heart as was ascribed to God.

The "desert fathers," of whom Saint Anthony is the primary representative, lived in remote places in the desert, in huts and caves. Their whole lives were directed toward seeking God through prayer, meditation, austerity, and manual work.

Long before their deaths, both confessors and ascetics were treated by people with the same deference usually accorded to martyrs. The "desert fathers" especially were consulted about matters of the soul, and seekers would undertake long journeys to the hermitages of these holy men in the hope of finding spiritual solace and answers to their questions.

THE WONDROUS POWERS OF HOLY RELICS

There still remained the question, however, of how the faithful could be absolutely certain of the purity of spirit of a living saint – how could anyone know whether or not the holy person had, in the privacy of his cave, surrendered to temptation? Whether confessors or ascetics, they were still human, and a greater proof of spiritual integrity was needed in order to quell that doubt. The proof, as it happened, came in the form of miracles. Personal reputation for holiness only partly guaranteed eligibility for the formation of a saint's cult; this worthiness was finally

Opposite : *Ancient frescoes adorn the walls of Saint Anthony's monastery by the Red Sea. Saint Anthony was the first of the "desert fathers" who left the world in order to seek communion with God in the desert. Above: Reliquary containing mummified head of Saint Oliver Plunkett, Archbishop of Armagh, in Saint Peter's Church, Drogheda, Ireland. Martyred on the scaffold in 1681, he was canonized in 1975. His body is in Downside Abbey in England.*

sealed by the number of miracles that occurred at the saint's shrine, or that were associated with his or her relics after death.

In 415 CE, for instance, the relics of Stephen of Jerusalem were discovered and subsequently distributed to various locations in Christendom, where churches were built to honor the saint. Soon rumors started circulating that the relics had the power to heal illness. Reports were written, and the saint's reputation for working miracles spread. The example of Saint Stephen is but one of many.

Wonders and miracles were proclaimed wherever there was a saint's tomb, with the consequence that the cult of the saints sank even deeper roots into the imagination of the people. Every Christian community had its own patron saint, plus a few more to answer the prayers of the people. With the passing of time the popularity of these saints grew almost out of control; it was like a frenzy. Wherever Christians went – to convert the Celts in Britain, the Gauls in France, or the Slavs in Eastern Europe – more holy shrines were built to honor this or that saint.

Opposite: *Saint Seirol's Well in Anglesey, Wales.* Below left: *Saint Levan's Well in Cornwall.* Below right: *Madron Well, also in Cornwall. Holy Wells were an important site of pilgrimage, for the waters blessed by the saints had curative powers. At Saint Levan's Well, for instance, the sick lay on these stone slabs all night in hope of a cure.*

Constantinople in the Christian East did not possess the same wealth of saintly relics as the lands that had belonged to the Western Roman Empire, and thus started importing them. They came from the Holy Land at first – the bodies of Saint Luke, Saint Andrew, and Saint Timothy were moved – and from anywhere else afterwards. The fourth century saw the beginning of a trade in holy relics which was to develop into a veritable battle of local churches for possession of wonder-working relics. Just as it was believed that the soul is present

Saint Edellienta's shrine in Cornwall, England. A book with hand-written requests by the sick and troubled is placed upon the tomb in the hope that the Saint's power will cure them.

in every part of the body, so people concluded that the saint's power was present in every relic, regardless of whether a particular part of the holy person's body was attached to the rest or not, or whether it was separated from the tomb.

The whole affair soon grew into a lucrative international financial enterprise, complete with thefts, counterfeits, and potentially embarrassing duplications. Two different churches claimed the body of Saint Luke, and at least ten displayed the head of John the Baptist. The great diversity of the relics collected by a single church is gloriously exemplified by the collection held at Reading Abbey, in England, in the twelfth century. The abbey possessed 242 items altogether, including the bones of Saints Aethelmod and Branwalator; a rib and another bone from Saint David; "some of Saint Petroc and some of the cloth in which he was wound;" a fragment of the tomb of Saint Edward the Confessor; bits of the Blessed Virgin's hair, her bed, and her belts; the hand of Saint James; the head of Saint Philip; and the head, jawbone, vestments, one rib, and some hair from Saint Brigid.

The faithful left donations at the saints' sanctuaries, and in some cases hostels were built to house the pilgrims on the site of particularly

miraculous relics. Annual celebrations were also held – and they still are – on the anniversary of the death of a saint, when it was believed that the remains renewed their power.

Although all this had very obvious and not so holy political and economic significance, it nevertheless reflected a sincere expression of devotion to the saintly figure. The importance given by the devotees to the relics drew attention to the saint as a source of miraculous power. This marked a new development in the symbolism of sainthood, as the faithful came to believe that the saint could intercede on their behalf with the Holy Father.

From the development of the power of saints spanning the period between the Roman Empire and late Middle Ages, we can draw some conclusions about the requirements needed for sainthood.

1. The saint had to have a widespread reputation among the people, especially for martyrdom, asceticism, and confession.
2. The stories and legends that developed around a holy personality, containing symbols for the faithful of heroic virtue, were highly important.
3. A reputation for performing miracles, whether during a saint's lifetime or through wonder-producing relics, was essential.

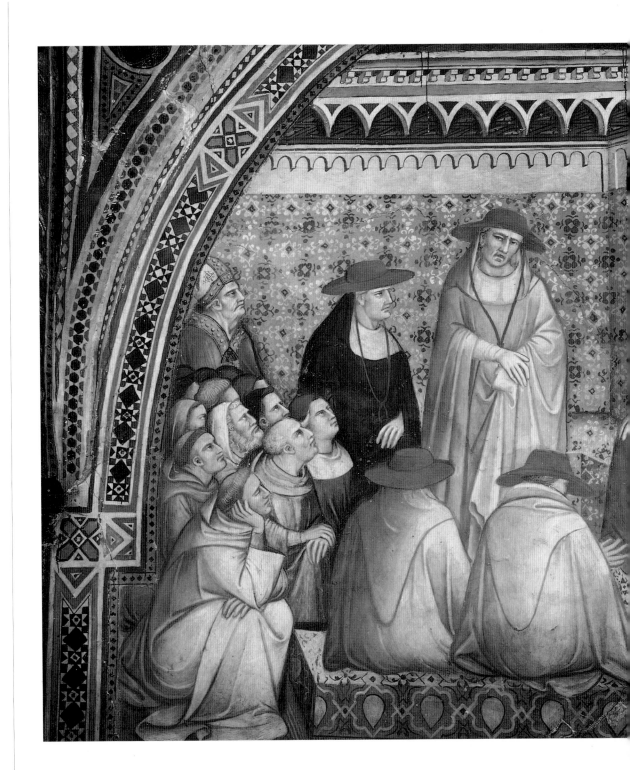

Pope Alexander III declared that no one, regardless of their reputation for holiness, could be worshipped without papal authorization. This painting is by Aretino Spinello (1332- c. 1410).

THE PATH TO OFFICIAL SAINTHOOD

The presence of a saint's entire body, or of a powerful relic, obviously enhanced the prestige of a particular church. Equally, the presence of a major shrine where miracles reputedly occurred enhanced all the churches of that area. The power and frequency of the miracles would attract a flow of pilgrims, many of whom would perhaps stay there for some time. Thus, the local bishops were particularly keen on supervising the shrines and holy relics in their dioceses for they had to make sure that these were "valid" objects of cult.

The masses of the faithful were so enamored of the saints that they frequently directed prayers to as many saints as they could remember. Their virtues were invoked, and their names read out loud so that everyone present at mass could honor the blessed. These lists of saints' names, called canons, were kept and renewed by the local dioceses and monasteries. The act of putting a saint's name into the canon is where the word "canonization" (declaring that someone is a saint) was originally used.

Obviously, with so many different local saints being proclaimed in different regions and countries, there was no way to determine how many saints there were at any given time, nor whether all these holy beings were in fact immaculately holy. The process of making saints had seemed until the fifth century a rather casual affair, brought about by popular pressure and rumors that miracles were happening. In effect, the person in question was proved to be a saint

SAINT DOMINIC,
FOUNDER OF THE ORDER OF THE PREACHERS

Dominic was born in Calaruega, in Spain, in 1170, of a Castilian family. When he was 26 years of age he became one of the canons at the cathedral in Osma. In 1206 his bishop, Diego, was appointed the official leader of a papal mission sent to convert the heretical Albigenses, who lived in Languedoc in southwestern France, and he chose Dominic as his companion. While in Languedoc they lived simply and discussed matters of faith with their opponents. These gentle methods contrasted with the usual formality and display of power which had characterized previous papal missions. When Bishop Diego died in 1207, some of the Albigenses murdered the papal legate Peter de Castelnau, and Pope Innocent II ordered a military campaign against their leader, Count Raymond of Toulouse. A bitter battle ensued which continued for five years, during which Dominic and his few followers still attempted to convert the "heretics."

In 1215 Dominic established his headquarters in Toulouse, and there founded an order of highly trained priests, bound by vows of poverty. The monastic order traveled and preached everywhere. The order was approved by Rome in 1216, and Dominic sent many brothers to the universities in Paris and Spain. He also emphasized the importance of women for his work and he established an order of nuns in San Sisto, Rome. The Dominican order spread worldwide thanks to the compassion of its founder for all kinds of human suffering. The saint is celebrated on the 4th day of August.

because so many people said so. However, the Church authorities argued that in their eagerness to believe, people were willing to attribute holiness to anything that was slightly out of the ordinary. And, additionally, who could prove that the miracles performed were not in fact the actions of the devil? There was no ready answer, apart from official supervision of the whole affair by the bishops themselves.

Thus, from the fifth to the tenth century, bishops gradually imposed a system of control over each case for sainthood presented to them. Before a new saint's name could be added to the now "official" canon, the authorities demanded proof in the form of written accounts of the person's life, virtues, death and possible martyrdom, as well as satisfactory reports – sometimes required from eyewitnesses – of any wondrous occurrence or miracles associated with the person in question. Once everything had been properly documented, the bishop would order the body to be exhumed from its tomb and transferred (called the "translation") to an altar, which in effect sealed the person's reputation as a saint. The next step was to assign a day on which the saint would be celebrated and his or her name added to the official Canon.

These measures, however, only established a person's reputation for holiness. They were useless when it came to proving a person's actual worthiness as an example for the faithful to imitate. Heretics who sought death because of some form of insanity or obsession could equally have been proclaimed saints, since the new procedures examined the martyrdom rather than the motives behind it. It became clear that more thorough control was needed when saintliness was at stake, and by the end of the tenth century the general consensus was that the Pope should, as the representative of God on earth, be responsible for declaring saints. However, it was a long time before the papacy took complete control of this delicate process, and the procedures to examine and assess sainthood were to be refined over the next seven centuries as the power of the papacy itself was strengthened.

In 1170, Pope Alexander III (1159-81) declared that no one, regardless of their reputation for holiness, miracles, and wondrous cures, could be prayed to without papal authorization. A saint was an object of veneration for the entire Church, and thus the Pope as the ultimate Church authority

was the one to decide whether a cult should be allowed or not. This statement obviously sent ripples of displeasure through the Catholic countries, especially those located north of the Alps. How could Rome, the northerners argued, ascertain the validity of saints whose cults had taken root centuries before? Who was the Pope going to send as his legate for the investigation, and how were they to conduct such an investigation into a matter which could be hundreds of years old? The first seeds of dissent that were to lead to the Reformation were planted in response to the way in which sainthood was legislated at this time.

Papal legates did indeed travel everywhere, and undertook serious investigations whenever a case for sainthood was presented by a local bishop. In addition, Rome took care not to allow any new cults to arise, prohibiting the publication of papers or books containing information on the person's reputed miracles and forbidding the public display of an individual's image with haloes or radiance around the head.

When the papacy moved from Rome to Avignon (1309-77) the Church underwent a process of bureaucratization which was to influence deeply the process of making saints. From then on, canonization became a legal procedure: the petitioners presenting the case for a particular saint were represented by a legal procurator who presented the case to the Church authorities, represented in their turn by the "Promoter of the

SAINT THOMAS AQUINAS

Thomas was born in Roccasecca, near Aquino, in 1225. He was one of the many children of Landulf of Aquino, a nobleman of Lombard descent. Thomas was educated by the Benedictines at Monte Cassino and in Naples, where in 1244 he joined the order. His family was so shocked at the news that he intended to become a mendicant friar that his brothers kidnapped him and locked him in a tower for a year. However, Thomas did not change his mind and the family finally released him. He subsequently went to study under Saint Albert the Great in Paris and Cologne, and 1256 he completed his degree in theology. The rest of Thomas' life was devoted to teaching and to writing – at the end of 1273 he left his great work, the Summa theologica, *which has been translated into twenty-two volumes, unfinished, declaring that, "All I have written seems to me like so much straw compared with what I have seen and with what has been revealed to me." He was asked to attend the council at Lyons, but he undertook the journey being already ill, and died at the abbey of Fossanuova in 1323. The* Summa theologica *earned him the name of "universal teacher;" the text is a systematic exposition of theology and has been studied since his time as a classic of enlightened thought. His influence on the Church and religious thought has been enormous. In 1567 he was declared a doctor of the Church by Pope Pius V. He is celebrated on the 7th day of March.*

The Triumph of Saint Thomas Aquinas by Francesco Traini.

SAINT FRANCIS OF ASSISI

Francesco Bernardone was born in Assisi, in the province of Perugia, Italy, in the year 1181. He was the son of a wealthy merchant draper, and as a youth led a frivolous, carefree life with friends in the local community. This simple, joyful existence ended when he was recruited to go to war. He was wounded in battle and returned home very ill. While recovering he awakened to the need for deeper religiousness in the world. One day in the church of San Damiano he heard an image of Christ say to him, "Francesco, repair my falling house." He took the words literally and, without asking permission, sold many of his father's goods in order to carry out the works to the church. His father, angry at what he considered Francesco's foolishness, disinherited and disowned him, and Francesco left home to "wed Lady Poverty." Many of his once reckless friends joined him and together they lived in poverty, chastity, and in faith in God. Three years later, in 1210, Pope Innocent III authorized Francesco and eleven companions to be wandering preachers of Christ. The headquarters of the brothers was the Porziuncola chapel at Santa Maria degli Angeli, on the outskirts of Assisi. The brothers traveled throughout Italy calling people to simplicity and repentance. In 1212 Francesco founded with Clare (who was canonized Saint Clare in 1255) the community of the Poor Ladies.

By 1217 the movement of the followers of Francesco was beginning to take the shape of a monastic order. So many members had joined that it became necessary to set up communities elsewhere in Italy, and some traveled to other parts of Europe. In 1221 Cardinal Ugolino, a friend of Francesco, revised the rule of the order, reiterating the vows of poverty, humility, and evangelical freedom which had characterized its founder. In 1224, while Francesco was praying on Monte La Verna in the Apennines, stigmata – bleeding scars corresponding to the five wounds inflicted on Jesus on the cross – appeared on his body. The stigmata never left him and caused great pain which made him suffer intensely until he met "Sister Death" in 1226.

Saint Francis of Assisi remains to this day one of the most popular saints of Christianity, and represents a model of simplicity, directness, and single-mindedness for many. He was not just an inspired mystic and individualist – his tremendous power and insight made him one of the best representatives of Christ. In 1979 Pope John Paul II proclaimed him patron saint of the ecologists, perhaps because during his life Saint Francis had addressed the natural world as his own kin. Many odes and songs have been composed to celebrate what St. Francis called Brother Sun and Sister Moon, Sister Water, and Brother Wolf. Many are still sung today by Franciscan monks and school children alike. His feast day is on the 4th of October.

A I N T S

Saint Francis of Assisi, inspired founder
of the evangelical Friars Minor or
"Lesser Brothers."*

Faith," who soon became popularly known as "The Devil's Advocate." Also, the Church demanded to see letters from individuals in positions of authority such as princes, kings, and high members of the Curia, recommending a certain petition as worthy of attention. This effectively meant that the evidence provided by ordinary people was no longer trusted, and that greater authority was needed to push a case forward to the starting point.

Saints, however, continued to be popular and more models of virtue arose throughout the centuries during which the process of canonization was being formalized. Mendicant orders such as that established by Saint Francis of Assisi, penitents who had converted from sin to virtue and now exemplified it for others to imitate, monastic reformers, and laity who worked among the poor and sick – names representing all these new "types" of heroic and religious virtue were being considered for official canonization.

The popular demand for saints soon became so great that the Church succumbed to the pressure by answering with a compromise: those individuals who had successfully received the seal of Church approval were to be called "sancti" (saints), while those who were venerated by the faithful, but had not received official recognition, were to be tolerated by the Church and could be called "beati" (blessed).

As the Church evolved, so the types of saints altered. Over time, the individuals chosen as suitable candidates for sainthood reflected more and more the needs of the papacy and of its supporters – chiefly the noble and princely houses of Europe. Centralized by the Pope in Rome, the power to canonize became the power to determine what sainthood was and what it should mean for the faithful. What interested the papacy was to provide models of moral conduct far surpassing that of most human beings – a saint needed to be extraordinary. Individuals who made vows of poverty, chastity, and obedience, and who chose paths of renunciation which sharply distinguished "religious" from "ordinary" life, were made saints. Such achievements, however, were very difficult to obtain outside monastic life. Thus, implicitly, the papacy defined the latter as being a "better" kind of existence, and the only avenue to holiness. With few exceptions, the path to sainthood

A portrait of Martin Luther, the powerful instigator of the Reformation, who called for a change in the medieval Catholic Church along simpler, purer, and more spiritual lines.

became an institutional process closed to ordinary folk. From the Middle Ages until today, very few Catholics who have not made vows of poverty, chastity, and obedience, have been proclaimed saints.

The new paradigm of sainthood, which seemed to be elevated farther and farther above ordinary life, did not, however, satisfy the needs of the faithful. The saints preferred in Rome were not popular among ordinary people, who wanted patrons for their towns and intercessors in heaven for their everyday human problems. While the papacy offered examples of high moral conduct, the people needed someone to invoke in curing an illness, or healing a broken love affair; someone to console them and restore their faith when their children died, someone to protect them from storms and natural cataclysms. Pope Innocent IV (1243-59) went as far as to declare that mere religious virtue was not enough to make someone a saint. Sanctity, he stated, required a life of "constant, uninterrupted virtue," which effectively meant perfection. Proof of virtue was not to be considered at all, unless it could be proven to be also "heroic." The tales of saints, as a consequence, began to portray people more and more devoid of their humanness. They were instead just empty vessels that could receive the divine presence.

Thus the tension within the Church itself grew, pulled as it was by two differing poles. The meaning and purpose of sainthood gradually shifted from being a popular phenomenon, in which miracles gave joy and a sense of faith, to a symbol of such high virtue it was practically impossible to reach. The only medieval saint to rise above this tension was Saint Francis of Assisi, a saint of the people.

THE PROTESTANT REFORMATION

The popular demand for and veneration of saints increased, in a sense, as the papacy imposed more and more exacting standards upon the issue of sainthood. People prayed to saints, swore by them, undertook pilgrimages, hoped for miracles. The literate read martyrologies and saints' biographies, and the unlearned worshipped statues and relics. The power ascribed to the saints, both from the Church and from the faithful's point of view, was immense – so much so that, if viewed from the outside, Christianity may have looked like a polytheistic religion not unlike Hinduism. The saints received as much veneration as God himself, if not more.

But a storm was gathering in northern Europe, which would effectively make the notion of sainthood sheer anathema to many branches of Christianity. Protestantism began in the sixteenth century as a

reaction to (and a protest against) the doctrines and practices of the medieval Roman Church.

At the time, the distinction between religion and magic was more than a little blurred. This was an attitude promoted by the medieval Catholic Church, whose priests were to go down in history for "selling places in Paradise and graces" for cash. Martin Luther (*c.* 1483-1546), Huldreich Zwingli (1484-1531) and others called for a reformation of Church creed along simpler, purer, and more spiritual lines. Rome, it was felt, promoted the Christian faith in such a way that it encouraged superstition and incantation.

In fact, the accusation that the Church was drenched from head to foot in magic of little spiritual value was to become the *pièce de résistance* of the Protestant Reformation. The early rebels protested against beliefs which were central to the Church rituals, starting with the "exorcisms" and blessings performed upon the holy water which, had they been effective, would have made it the best curative drink for any illness. The fact that these rituals were mostly ineffective, the reformers argued,

meant that they should be abolished altogether. They also protested against the rituals promulgated by the Church that suggested its protection was indispensable to human survival, such as the consecration of church bells against tempests. They also objected to practices such as the wearing of words from scriptures against danger, and the fact that priests believed themselves to be magicians performing spells during mass, uttering words which they believed had a certain magical power.

Early Protestantism thus denied the magic of the "opus operatum", the claim that the Church had instrumental power and had been endowed by Christ with an active share in his work. The saints – not unnaturally, given their importance in the popular imagination – also came under attack. The reformers believed that it was blasphemy for human authority to claim the power to work miracles – this was a challenge to God's omnipotence. The saints were seen as remnants of a kind of paganism which had been perpetuated under a Christian veneer. The liberal reform ridiculed the popular and cultish belief in the saints, their relics, and religious pilgrimages, seeking instead to reinstate a wholehearted faith in God alone. The reformers moreover, starting with Martin Luther, rejected the hierarchical structure of the Church; this effectively meant that the social and political influence of Rome was rejected as well.

The immediate effect of the Reformation on those churches where their influence was strongest was the collapse of the cult of the saints. Their statues and relics disappeared from every reformed church. Martin Luther, among others, rejected the notion of the saint as intercessor between mankind and God, and thought that the cult of the saints was blasphemous and idolatrous. Thus the cult of the saints disappeared from Protestant Christianity, and only survives within the Roman Catholic Church.

At the time of the Reformation, the Papists responded to the rebellion with a reaffirmation of the cult of the saints, which was a tradition perhaps too ancient and too dear to be abandoned altogether. But the Church did undertake several important reformations of its own which effectively put the affair of canonization under tighter control. Pope Urban VIII (1623-44) wrote down the rules and laws that were to govern the process of making saints for the centuries to come.

THE PROCESS OF CANONIZATION

Even though the ultimate judgment of whether an individual should be beatified or canonized rests with the Pope, the procedure for making saints is allocated to a lesser authority within the Vatican – "The Congregation for the Causes of Saints" – whose job it is to investigate each case and ascertain whether the person in question is in fact worthy of sainthood. This process is painstakingly lengthy and detailed, for, we must remember, the Congregation is ultimately trying to assess whether an individual has been chosen by God to perform His work on earth. The process is entirely based upon the laws of jurisprudence, and is typically divided into different stages of assessment. We can take a look at the different stages of the process, and thereby see just how complex it is, though in its way it has a certain exalted fascination.

The first step towards holiness is taken when the friends of the deceased, believing there is a case for sanctity, literally initiate a promotion to make their belief known. A guild, named after the saint-to-be, is formed to gather reports on divine favors credited to the individual. A newsletter commemorating the person's virtues is circulated. All this is intended to alert the bishop of the local diocese and to promote a private cult of the deceased.

If the local bishop agrees that there are good grounds

for sanctification, he opens an official enquiry into the person's life and deeds. A group of officials, named the "College of Relators," compiles a historical biography of the so-called "Servant of God" which functions very much like a doctoral dissertation. Witnesses may be called upon to give evidence, but the bulk of the information is derived from historical research. Part of the enquiry may entail exhuming the corpse for identification. If the body should happen not to be corrupted – and this occasionally does occur – then the cause is greatly enhanced. The Roman Catholic Church however, unlike the Russian Orthodox Church, does not regard an uncorrupted body as confirmation of sanctity, because such a condition might have resulted from environmental factors. Until relatively recently, however, it was believed that the "odor of sanctity" – a sweet scent that is said to emanate from a saint's corpse – could lead the bishops to support the cause of a true saint without further ado.

Another very important and still more dramatic element in the enquiry is proof that the saint-to-be has performed miracles, for the very definition of sainthood implies such powers. And it is at this most important and delicate stage that the College of Relators must determine whether the candidate has been chosen by God to do His work on earth or not. If all the facts that have been established in building the candidate's reputation for holiness are seen to be extraordinary, but still not outside human achievement, then there is need for proof of divine intervention.

This part of the process could be described as truly metaphysical, resting, as it does, somewhere between science and mythology. First of all it must be established that God truly performed a miracle and, secondly, that the miracle occurred through the intercession of the candidate. A panel of medical experts is called to determine whether the miracle –very often a healing – might have occurred for natural or medically explainable reasons. Once a positive verdict is reached, then the material is turned over to theological experts who judge whether the miracle truly occurred through the intercession of the candidate, and not, as might be the case, through prayers given to another saint. When all the "facts" have been verified and certified, the information is circulated through the higher ranks of the Congregation and eventually the Pope issues a formal decree of acceptance of the miracle.

A minimum of two miracles are needed for

Mother Teresa of Calcutta is here presented with a chalice in honor of her support of a charity house in China. Mother Teresa is a saint of the people, representing a powerful paradigm of modern spirituality and a living example for many.

a mass are established to honor the "blessed Servant of God."

Beatification, however gratifying, is not the last step. To underline this point, the Pope himself does not attend the mass honoring the blessed, but comes in afterwards to make a speech on the virtues of the Servant of God.

Unless there are more divine signs after beatification, the cause might lie dormant for decades. If, however, miracles do occur, and thus there are good grounds to believe that God continues to work through the blessed individual, a new inquiry is set up to seek real proof. Once the last miracle is examined and approved – only two miracles are needed after beatification – then the cause reaches its last stage. The Pope issues a decree for canonization in which it is declared that the blessed Servant of God must be venerated as a saint throughout all the Catholic churches in the world.

The fact that the Roman Catholic Church still continues to discover and proclaim saints underscores the faithful's ever present need for guidance. The process of making saints, however lengthy and juridical it may seem, is a well-oiled machine which has been developed for over four centuries. It is hoped that with so much practice, the machine will be tuned to the emerging awareness of what sanctity needs to represent in this age of expanding global consciousness.

beatification, and two more for canonization if the cause is based on virtue. If the candidate has been martyred, then no proof of miracles is needed, for the sacrifice of a life in the name of God is sufficient to prove sanctity. Once all the material has been gathered, a dissertation is given on the heroic virtue or martyrdom of a candidate in front of the cardinals and the official prelates belonging to the Congregation for the Causes of Saints. They then pass a judgment at a formal meeting held at the Apostolic Palace.

If the cause can safely result in a decree for beatification then an apostolic brief is issued in which the Pope proclaims that the candidate can be worshipped as one of the Church's "blessed." The veneration is, however, restricted to the particular region, country, or religious order where the petition for sainthood was initiated. Also, a special prayer and

CHAPTER THREE

THE JEWISH CASE

he notion of individual sainthood in Judaism is problematic, and it almost poses a contradiction in terms. The fundamental belief, very simplistically expressed here, is that the entire Jewish nation is chosen by God to be a "light unto the gentiles," a choice which is ratified by covenant. By practicing his or her faith the Jewish individual is working towards the redemption of the whole people, towards the creation of a just and holy society. There are no saints' feasts in the Jewish religious calendar, nor any official recognition that an individual might intercede in heaven on behalf of mankind. Because the Jews believe redemption will come only when the people as a whole are ready for it, no amount of isolated individual effort will cause it to happen. On the contrary, individual effort is simply part of performing one's duty to fulfill God's commandments.

Within the parameters of the Orthodox Jewish community, there are three ideals of spirituality which can be cultivated by the individual for the common good. The first is represented by the "talmid hakham," or scholar of the rabbinical tradition. Starting as the student of a sage, the talmid hakham continues to study the Torah, the Scriptures and Law, all his life. Because the Torah has been dictated by God, the study of it puts the scholar in direct touch with God's thoughts and intentions. Since ancient times, the rabbinic sage has been the model of religiousness in Judaism, as well as being a source of great wisdom for the community who

Opposite: *Moses and the Burning Bush, by William Blake. Moses is a figure of awesome importance in the Jewish tradition, for he was the first to know God face to face.* Below: *An illuminated page from a medieval "siddur," the Hebrew book of prayer.*

have looked to him for advice in matters great and small.

The later ideal of religious leader is represented by the "tsaddiq," or righteous person. The tsaddiq differs from the talmid hakham in that it is not his knowledge, but his life that endows him with religious value. The tsaddiq is a man free from sin, who practices charity and obeys the Torah. He becomes the living incarnation of the Torah, and benefits the world at large as well as himself. This merit is believed to have been shared by the patriarchs such as Moses, who sustained Israel through its tribulations. Martyrs and those persecuted for being Jews are also considered tsaddiqim. The Talmudic rabbis hold the righteous in such high esteem that they believe that a certain number of them (between thirty and forty-five) per generation will outweigh the world's sins. In fact, an ancient Hebrew legend tells that there are "thirty-six just men" who sustain the world.

The third model of spirituality is represented by the "hasid" (literally "pious one"), a devotee who seeks his own mystic path to the attainment of unity with God. This person goes beyond scholarly knowledge of the Torah, and seeks an individual experience of the divine presence. The hasid's aim is to live in accordance with Jewish doctrine out of pure love, and when his heart is aflame with such love he is deemed worthier than a scholar.

These three ideals are in reality intertwined: the sage is, as a consequence of his wisdom, a righteous individual and, inevitably, a lover of God. Remarkable men incarnating these qualities are celebrated within the heart of Jewish mysticism. They represent examples of a living religion and, despite discord with rabbinical doctrine, they are considered "saints" within our broader definition of the term.

Opposite: *King David holding the scrolls of the Law, by Marc Chagall.* Right: *A wood engraving illustrating one of the many stories surrounding the Ba'al Shem Tov, founder of the Hasidic movement.*

THE HASIDIC MOVEMENT

Several powerful examples of spirituality and mysticism are found at the periphery of mainstream Judaism, namely within the heart of the Hasidic movement which has inspired thousands of individual Jews. The main characteristic of the movement is its celebration of God's presence in everyday life: worship, prayer and ritual punctuate the existence of the individual, of the family, and of the community. For the Hasid, God is ever-present, and through constant communion and centering the mind upon Him, the individual can be transformed.

The Hasidic movement originated around the middle of the eighteeth century in what was then known as the Polish Kingdom, which at the time included Lithuania, Belorussia, and the Ukraine. Its founder was the charismatic Israel ben Eleazar (1700-60), known to his followers as the Ba'al Shem Tov, or "Master of the Good Name"– meaning, in other words, the possessor of the secret of the ineffable name of God. He was a miracle-worker and visionary who claimed access to a heavenly teacher, the prophet Ahijah. What he offered to his followers was a way to redemption through the ecstatic experience of God in all things. Individuals, by sanctifying the everyday world around them, could serve God with joy.

The main contribution of the Ba'al Shem Tov was to deliver classical teachings by means of fables and parables drawn from both daily life and folklore. This method appealed greatly to the Jewish masses, and presented a "living Torah" which could be experienced through his personality. He taught that God's closeness was accessible to all.

THE MAGGID OF MEZERITCH

The Maggid of Mezeritch was born in 1710, ten years after the Ba'al Shem Tov, into a poor family in Volhynia in eastern Poland, south of Lithuania. He married young and earned a meager living as a school teacher. He was also a Talmudic scholar and a mystic, and the rigors he subjected himself to in order to cultivate virtue made him disapproving of the ecstatic ways of the Ba'al Shem. He fell gravely ill as a consequence of the penitence he inflicted upon his body and, after several doctors had been unable to help him, someone suggested he visit the Ba'al Shem Tov. The Maggid did this, was unimpressed, and was about to return home when a messenger arrived and urged him to go back to the Ba'al Shem.

Having come this far, the Maggid thought that he might as well give the healer a second chance, even though it was late at night. The Ba'al Shem gave him the "Book of Splendor," the Zohar, to read, and as he showed him how to read the holy words with the fullness of his soul, the room was filled with light and the Maggid felt as though he were on Mount Sinai receiving the word of God from the burning bush. Thus he was convinced of the holiness of the Ba'al Shem Tov and became his disciple and later his successor.

The Maggid of Mezeritch's fame was such that many came to him to learn. He helped them discover depths within themselves that they had never felt before, and ascend to heights which they had never before attained. He established a Hasidic network spanning the whole of Eastern Europe so that the flame kindled by the Ba'al Shem Tov made its way to thousands of individuals. Every community had at its head a rabbi, also called a tsaddiq, whose task it was to keep the spirit of the Ba'al Shem alive among the people. The Maggid understood the importance of transmitting the teachings, and one of his greatest attributes was his ability to communicate them to many others. Many of his disciples became spiritual leaders themselves and founded new Hasidic communities.

Above: *A prayer ball, depicting communal scenes.*
Opposite: *Rabbi Schneerson, revered head of the Lubavitch Foundation, a branch of the Hasidic movement.*

After the death of the Ba'al Shem Tov his disciples dispersed and became tsaddiqim, leaders of new Hasidic communities. These growing centers of spiritual inspiration attracted many who found in each individual tsaddiq a specific orientation and interpretation of the doctrine. The tsaddiqim of the Hasids also reached the souls of devotees by praying with and for them, answering their questions, and curing their spiritual ills. They were seen as exemplars, as unique manifestations of the Torah. They were channels through which divine power flowed to the community and divine agents through which the community could contact God. In other words, they were saints.

One Hasidic doctrine teaches that the tsaddiq is a light so powerful as to be able to lift up the souls of those around him. Although the tsaddiq's inner self is bound with God, he goes out to people to feel their pain and sorrow, in order to lead them from their earthly predicament to the highest levels of spiritual attainment.

In the contemporary world the tsaddiqim continue to function and are venerated among Hasidim as living saints, despite Judaism's traditional antipathy towards the concept. Their main function is to transmit the ancient teachings that were passed to the Jewish people directly from God. In Hebrew the word "massora," meaning tradition, comes from the verb "limsor," meaning "to transmit," and it is this tradition of transmission which forms the kernel of Jewish wisdom and practice. Just as within the Hasidic movement the teaching is passed from generation to generation through the personae of the tsaddiqim, from one being to another, so in traditional Judaism the flame is rekindled in the stories of those great and holy individuals who carried out God's plan.

S   A   I   N   T   S

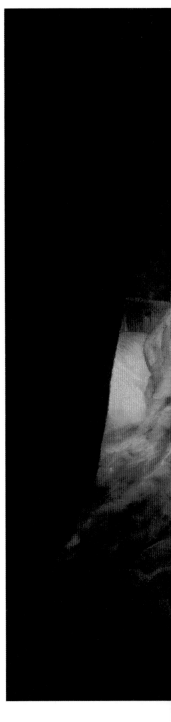

THE PATRIARCHS AS MODELS OF INSPIRATION

In Jewish terms, the presence of God has been experienced throughout history, starting with the first man and woman, Adam and Eve. His presence is felt in the natural realm, but more poignantly in His intimate and immediate participation in human life. Other ancient communities in northern Mesopotamia (where the family of the original Patriarch is believed to have originated in the mid-second millennium BCE) shared the belief of the presence of a god in their everyday existence. But this concept was taken to greater depths by the early Hebrews, and forms the focus of Jewish religious affirmation.

One of the main characteristics of Judaism is exactly the intimate relationship of His people with their God. The fundamental qualities espoused by the first patriarchs – of wisdom, obedience, and morality – have been passed on from generation to generation for nearly 4,000 years. The patriarchs, although not considered saints, are nevertheless models of inspiration for all Jews. Their stories are familiar to everyone, and form a mystical link between present-day Jews and their ancient forefathers, tracing a direct line of inheritance which bridges millennia.

Above: A silver plate depicting Abraham about to sacrifice his son Isaac on Mount Moriah in a test of his faith. Right: Jacob blessing the children of Joseph, by Rembrandt.

82

ABRAHAM

Abraham is the legendary first father of the Israelites, more historical perhaps than the Biblical father of mankind, Adam. According to the Book of Genesis, Abraham, with his father Terah and his nephew Lot, left his native city Ur, in Mesopotamia, at a time of political trouble caused by the collapse of the empire of Babylon. They traveled northwest to Haran, between the Euphrates and the Tigris rivers, near the frontier of modern-day Turkey and Syria. When they had settled in Haran, Abraham's father Terah died and God called Abraham to resume his travels. So Abraham set out once more with his wife Sarah, his nephew Lot, and other companions south into the land of Canaan. There God appeared to him and told him that his "seed" would inherit the land, and Abraham built an altar to the Lord at Moreh, near Shechem. In time, a famine wiped out his flocks and herds, and drove him and his companions farther south into Egypt.

Now Abraham's wife, Sarah, was very beautiful. Because he was afraid that the pharaoh of Egypt would try to steal Sarah by killing him, Abraham pretended that she was his sister. The pharaoh was in fact so enchanted by Sarah that he took her into his palace and awarded Abraham with many good things; however, God inflicted many diseases upon Pharaoh and his court. When Pharaoh discovered Abraham's lie, he returned Sarah to him and ordered them to leave the country. God guided Abraham back to Canaan and promised again that he would become the founder of a new nation. Abraham obeyed the commands of God unquestioningly.

Once in Canaan, Abraham sought to create a dynasty, but had no legitimate heir, and as Sarah was still childless she gave him her servant Hagar as a concubine. Hagar gave birth to a son called Ishmael. Thirteen years later, God promised to fulfill His covenant and to give Abraham offspring who would inherit the land, on condition that he and all his descendants should be circumcised as a sign of that covenant. One day, three men appeared to Abraham as he was sitting outside his tent and announced that his wife would bear him a son. Sarah overheard them and laughed, for she was by then well past childbearing age. However, soon afterward she conceived and gave birth to Isaac, whose name means "laughter" or "joy." Abraham was later commanded by God to sacrifice his son Isaac on Mount Moriah as a test of his faith. He was about to kill Isaac when an angel appeared and told him to sacrifice a ram instead, which was caught by the horns in a nearby bush.

In his old age, Abraham bought the cave of Machpelah at Hebron where he buried Sarah and was himself later buried by his sons Isaac and Ishmael. This place is still venerated today.

Opposite: *An illuminated page from the manuscript of the Pentateuch, showing a medieval Jewish school.* Below: *A vanitas painting by Benjamin Senior Godines, depicting harmony and beauty.*

WALKING GOD'S WAY

The Jewish people have been confronted by the person of God on numerous occasions; God is there to help and guide in times of trouble, and individuals are expected to be as moral in their dealings with each other as God is toward the community at large. Thus the only acceptable behavior is to walk in "God's way," helping others in times of need and struggle and strengthening the sense of community in everyday life. This principle is nowhere made more clear and vibrant than in the person of Moses. His character, life, and deeds represent the highest ideals that Jews can aspire to.

When Moses entered into direct contact with God on Mount Sinai, God confirmed His intervention in history. The Israelites had been chosen to fulfill His purposes, and the terms of His covenant would regulate their conduct to make them a holy nation – a spiritual community serving as an example for the rest of the world. The liberation from Egypt, the journey

to the promised land, and the continued sustenance of His people, were based upon the obligation of their exclusive loyalty to Him – thus, traditionally, festivals commemorate God's bounty and help rather than individual human feats by the patriarchs. God is the teacher of mankind. He gives guidance and instruction in the form of laws (the Torah) that regulate both the human and moral conduct of His people. The duty of the Jewish people at large is thus to fulfill their promise and create a perfected society that fits with God's vision. As redeemer, God will one day become incarnate on earth and enable the whole of mankind to experience divine perfection.

An extraordinary level of maturity is required of every Jew in order to fulfill God's plan; maturity and awareness must be exerted in the small things of everyday life, as well as in the greater socio-political order. Jewish history has given birth to a number of

Opposite: *Children celebrating Hanukkah, the Festival of Lights.* Below: *In Jerusalem, it has now become a popular custom to hold bar mitzvah celebrations by the Wall.*

Right: *Moses and the Brazen Serpent, by Sir Anthony Van Dyck, Museo del Prado, Madrid.* Below: *Moses performs a miracle by bringing forth water out of a rock. The painting is by Filippino Lippi, in the National Gallery, London.*

MOSES

Following famine and drought in Canaan, the nomadic Israelites sought refuge in Egypt where they settled. Here they prospered and multiplied and aroused the envy of the pharaohs who subjected them to slavery. The pharaoh at the time of Moses' birth had decided that the Israelites posed a threat and so ruled that all their newborn male children should be killed by being thrown into a river. When Moses was born his parents, Amram and Jochebed, hid him for three months and then wrapped him in a reed basket and set him afloat on the Nile.

The child was found by Pharaoh's daughter while she was bathing in the river, and she took him to her father's court where he was raised as an Egyptian prince. When Moses was a young man he discovered that he was a Hebrew and decided to look into the conditions under which his people were living. When he went to a site where they were laboring as slaves, he saw a taskmaster beating a fellow Hebrew to death. Unable to control his anger, Moses killed the Egyptian overlord. Fearful that Pharaoh would hear of his crime, Moses fled to the land of Midian, on the northeastern shores of the Red Sea.

While he was resting by a well, the seven daughters of the Midianate priest Jethro came to draw water for their father's flocks. Other shepherds arrived and rudely drove the girls away from the well in order to water their own flocks. Moses, again enraged by injustice, fought off the shepherds and helped the girls. Eventually he came to marry one of them, Zipporah, and assumed responsibility for Jethro's flocks. The prince now lived as a bedouin, roaming the wilderness in search of good pastures. One day his attention was attracted by a flaming bush which did not seem to be consumed by the fire burning it. As he approached the bush to investigate this odd phenomenon, he was warned by a voice not to come any closer and to remove his sandals before stepping upon holy ground. The voice, which seemed to come from the flaming bush, was the voice of the God of his forefathers, of Abraham, Isaac, and Jacob. It urged him to deliver the Hebrews from slavery.

Moses was reluctant to accept the call of God, doubting that he was capable of accomplishing such a feat. But God reassured him, saying that he and the children of Israel would one day worship Him upon that very mountain. Moses thus returned to Egypt to fulfill God's commandment. He first tried diplomacy, telling Pharaoh of God's wish to have the people of Israel liberated, but the sovereign refused. Moses then sought the help of God, who sent ten successive plagues to punish the arrogance of Egypt. After the last, most terrible plague – the death of all firstborn Egyptian children – Pharaoh relented. Moses led his people out of enslavement through a long and arduous journey across the desert. In the third month of their wanderings, the Israelites reached Mount Sinai, where the divinity had first spoken to Moses in the form of the flaming bush. Moses ascended the mountain and amid cataclysmic natural phenomena, God spoke to him again. He gave him the ten commandments in the form of two tablets of stone written "with God's finger," and instructions for the making of an ark to contain the tables of the law and God's covenant with Abraham.

Subsequently the people were guided towards their promised land, the land of Canaan.

The place of Moses in the history of Israel is second to none. He was the first to know God face to face, to accept His overpowering call to mission. He brought to the people of Israel the revelation of God's law on Sinai and the Covenant binding them to observe His ethical and moral code. The Promised Land was to be more than a place to inhabit in freedom; it was to be the earthly model of a divinely ordained society.

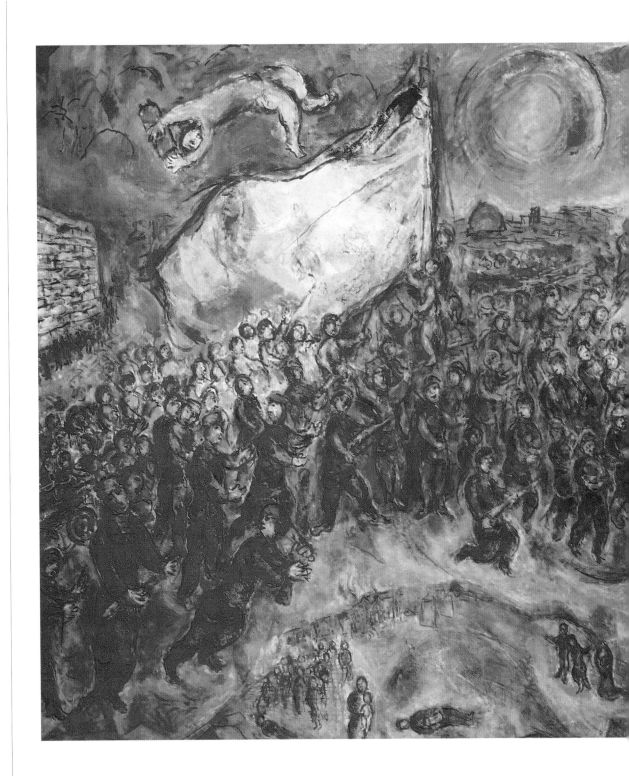

The Prophecy of Isaiah, by Marc Chagall; private collection, Saint Paul de Vence.

exceptionally gifted individuals – the prophets – whose inspired vision has led the way at different times towards the fulfillment of the Hebrew dream. The prophets combined God-endowed foresight with courage, strength of character, and illuminated thinking – gifts which morally sustained the people through the hazards of their history. God had given the prophets the ability to discern the path towards perfection and to show it to their fellow men. They were divinely compelled to proclaim what was coming, and part of their revelation of the future was the denunciation of present evils – if the future was dark in the prophetic vision it was because the Israelites had abandoned the monotheism demanded

ELIJAH

Elijah, one of the first prophets, lived in the ninth century BCE in the northern Kingdom of Israel. He was the champion of the Jewish religion against rival Canaanite cults. He attacked King Ahab and his Phoenician queen Jezebel for importing the cult of Baal and his consort Astarte into Israel. Elijah's message was needed in order to bring the wavering people of Israel back to their true faith. God himself was believed to have sustained and provided for Elijah during the time when the country was damaged by devastating famine and drought. At His bidding Elijah, who was in danger for his speeches had angered the king and queen, hid by a brook named Cherith and there was miraculously fed by ravens (Cherith is a small tributary east of the river Jordan, about halfway between the Sea of Galilee and the Dead Sea). He was also mysteriously directed to a widow near Sidon whose child he rescued from death by prayer.

Elijah's faith was manifested most dramatically when he persuaded Ahab to assemble 450 priests of Baal on Mount Carmel in a contest to ignite a sacrificial bull by invoking their respective gods. In spite of much capering and self-mutilation, the priests of Baal were totally unsuccessful and failed in the challenge. Elijah, on the other hand, succeeded in igniting the offering, thus demonstrating the power of the God of Israel. Soon after this miracle, the drought was broken by great rains. Ahab was thus put to shame and Jezebel, his wife, vowed vengeance on Elijah. He fled to Beersheba in the southern Kingdom of Judah and deep into the desert beyond. On Mount Sinai God came to him in a still, small voice, and told him to consecrate Elisha as his successor, and to anoint Hazael and Jehu as kings-to-be of Syria and Israel who would kill Ahab and all the worshippers of Baal. Elijah performed the first of these tasks, but left the others to Elisha. Elijah did not die a natural death, but was instead whirled up to heaven by a great wind in a chariot and horses of fire – an ascent imbued with mystical significance. Today, Elijah is remembered at the feast of Passover.

Opposite: *Elijah's Sacrifice, by Albert Moore, Bury Art Gallery and Museum.*
Below: *The ascent of the Prophet Elijah, Russian School, Museum of the History of Religion, St. Petersburg.*

Left: *Carrying the scrolls of the Law during the Sabbath service, by William Rothenstein.* Opposite: *The menorah depicted in a Hebrew Bible from Spain, 1476.*

by God; the prophets' reverberating message invoked the prohibition on the people to worship any other god than their own, and equally dismissed any other god than their own as being no god at all.

The first prophets insisted on the unity of the twelve tribes of Israel and on the worship of the Hebrew God, thus establishing the essential prerequisites for and chief characteristics of the Israelites' impact upon the world that surrounded them.

The ancient prophets gave the Hebrew religion a spiritual dimension which transcended the initially contractual nature of its moral code. The phrase "the Law and the Prophets" became the standard way of referring to the code of behavior, legal and spiritual, by which all Jews must live. The prophets are still seen today as the milestones of morality, integrity, and spirituality which sustain the faith and advance the Jew's achievement of God's vision.

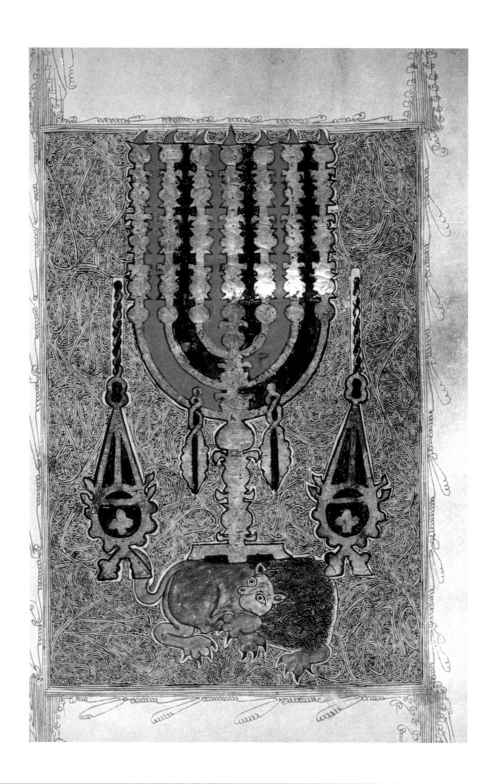

Below: *Muhammad and his companions.*
Opposite: *The minaret of a Moroccan mosque, from which the faithful are called to prayer five times a day.*

CHAPTER FOUR

THE WONDERS OF ISLAM

"God is most great.
I testify that there is no god but God.
I testify that Muhammad is the Messenger of God.
Come to prayer.
Come to salvation.
God is most great.
There is no god but God."

his "adhan," or public call to prayer by the muezzin, is made from the minaret of the mosque five times a day, summoning all Muslims to worship (the "Salat"). In the monotheism of Islam Allah is the only God, the Prophet Muhammad is His divinely sent Messenger, and the verses of the Koran (the "suras") are the divinely inspired teaching revealed to mankind through Muhammad. Thus, belief in God and in his final Messenger Muhammad makes up the essential confession of faith reaffirmed daily by all Muslims.

As he was chosen to be the channel of the last divine revelation, superseding all others, Muhammad, although a man, stood in a unique relationship with Allah. He represents to the faithful the paradigm of human virtue that all Muslims should cultivate. Islam, in fact, means "submission" to God, and in following their path all Muslims enjoy the blessings bestowed upon them by God.

Monotheism and the status accorded to the Prophet are absolutely central to Islam. As a consequence, belief in saints and holy beings who

Calligraphic motif: "Allah the Generous."

The Prophet Muhammad

Muhammad was born in Mecca c. 570 CE after the death of his father. He was first cared for by his grandfather, but as the climate in Mecca was thought to be unhealthy for a small baby, he was given to a wet nurse from a nomadic tribe living in the desert. When he was six years old his mother Aminah died, and when he was eight his grandfather, who had been a prominent politician of Mecca, died also. Muhammad was then raised by his uncle, Abu Talib, who took him on long trading journeys to Syria.

In 595 Muhammad was in charge of the merchandise of a wealthy woman, Khadijah, and he so impressed her that she offered marriage. She bore him two sons who died very young, and four daughters, of whom the most famous is Fatimah, the wife of Muhammad's cousin Ali, who is regarded as Muhammad's divinely ordained successor by the Shi'ah branch of Islam.

Muhammad took to spending nights in a hill cave near Mecca. There he pondered the problems which were afflicting Mecca: tribal solidarity was breaking up, and rich merchants preferred to pursue individual interests rather than fulfill their duties towards the more unfortunate. One day Muhammad had a vision of a majestic being and heard a voice saying to him, "You are the Messenger of God." This was the beginning of his vocation as Prophet of God. From this time onward, at frequent intervals until his death, he received "revelations" – messages that came directly from God. In about 650 CE the messages were collected and written down in the Koran, the sacred scriptures of Islam.

As Muhammad started to preach the new religion, he gathered followers who accepted his claim as Prophet of God. The religion was eventually called Islam, meaning "surrender to the will of God," and its followers Muslims, meaning "those who have surrendered."

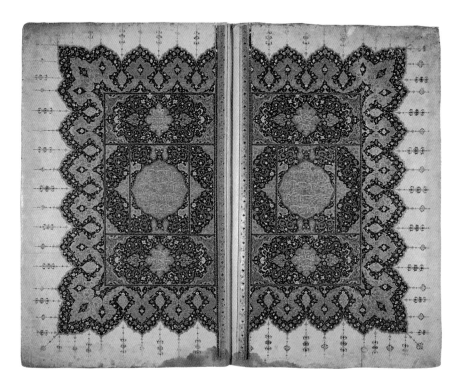

intercede with Allah on behalf of humankind, or who represent divine qualities on earth, would be a denial of these central precepts. In pure Islam the Prophet is the only worthy exemplar, and the source of inspiration in periods of crisis and renewal. A cult of saints, in other words, would be non-Islamic and intrinsically alien to the faith.

The words "holy" and "sacred" are eminently rare in the Islamic-Arabic vocabulary in specific reference to people, and they are sparse even when speaking of God. Thus, when we speak of saints in an Islamic context we must always remember that at root this is an alien concept which has been borrowed from other religions. In fact, the word that is most often translated as "saint" is the Arabic "wali" which means "friend," or "one who is near." All who obey God are walis, who in turn is wali to them. Both Jews and Christians are castigated in the Koran for asserting that they are special friends to God in an exclusive sense (62:6, 5:56). If there is one unforgivable sin in

Above: The frontispiece of a Koran, 1550. The holy book contains the final revelation of the truth by Allah to humanity. Below: The word that is most readily translated as "saint" within the Islamic context is "wali," meaning "friend" or "benefactor." Opposite: Dome of the Rock, Jerusalem. The magnificent Omayyad shrine built over the great rock Al Sakhra, venerated by Muslims as the site of the Prophet's ascension to heaven.

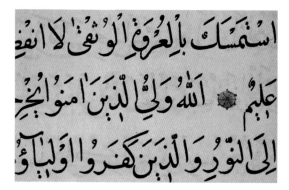

Below: *Illuminated manuscript painting of the Ka'bah at Mecca, Islam's most sacred place.* Opposite: *The thirteenth-century Sufi poet and mystic, Rumi, outside a blacksmith's shop.*

Islam it is that of associating anything or anyone with God, apart from the Prophet Muhammad, who is the only one who can intercede with Allah on behalf of humans.

Islam does, of course, possess the notion of virtue and "holiness." There are certain qualities that can be earned by an individual during his lifetime, and others which may be attributed by religious tradition. Any person, for instance, may become a religious scholar and thus earn the title of "shaikh."

Muslims are required to make at least one pilgrimage to Mecca during their lives, after which they may be called "hajji." Warriors ("ghazi") and martyrs ("shahid") also earn special titles. Depth of faith and the absolute cultivation of it, on the other hand, may earn a religious person the title of "murshid" (spiritual guide), "nabi" (prophet), or "mujjadid" (renewer of religion). A religious renewer is a particularly worthy person for he will keep the flame of the faith alight. While other sacred scriptures,

HASAN OF BASRA

Al-hasan ibn Abi 'l Hasan al-Basri was born in Medina in 642 CE, the son of a slave. Brought up in Basra, he met many companions of the Prophet and himself became one of the most prominent figures of his generation.

When he was a young man Hasan was a jewel merchant and was known by everyone as Hasan of the Pearls. He traded with Byzantium and was familiar with the generals and ministers of the Emperor. One day, one of the ministers commanded Hasan to follow him to a tent in the desert. There Hasan saw that a mighty army came, circled the tent, said a few words, and departed. Then, four hundred philosophers and scholars arrived, circled the tent, said a few words, and departed. They were followed by three hundred illuminated elders with white beards who also circled the tent, said a few words, and departed. Thereafter, two hundred moon-fair maidens, each bearing a plate of gold and silver and precious stones, repeated the motions Hasan had seen everyone else perform.

Filled with wonder Hasan asked the minister what this tent might be. The minister said that the Emperor had had a son of unsurpassable beauty, intelligence, and prowess. His father had loved him with all his heart. The son, however, had fallen suddenly very ill and all the physicians who were most skilled failed to cure him. Finally he had died and had been buried in that tent. The Emperor was so greatly saddened that he had arranged for armies, philosophers, venerable elders, and rich maidens to visit the burial place once a year. All their powers combined, said the minister, however great, had been unable to prevent the circumstances that had befallen the Emperor's son; someone of far greater power had sent an illness to kill him.

Hasan was so affected by the majesty of what he had seen that he was beside himself. At once he took an oath never to laugh again until his destiny became clear to him. He devoted himself to the study of holy scriptures and to all manner of austerities so as to become worthy of that great power which commanded the fate of mankind. No one surpassed his discipline and he became a great saint.

Right: *Suleymaniye mosque in Istanbul, founded by Sultan Suleyman (1520-66). Painted in Istanbul by European artists for a Western readership, the calls to prayer of the muezzins from the minarets are given in transliterated Arabic.*
Bottom: *Arabic calligraphy. "The Holy Prophet has said: 'Seek knowledge from the cradle to the grave.'"*

قال رسول الله : اُطلبوا العلم من المهد الى اللحد

such as the Bible and the New Testament, eagerly remind the reader of the unholiness and state of sin of all mankind, the Koran encourages the faithful to rejoice in the bounty which has been given to them.

Popular faith, however, needs perhaps more space than that afforded by the official parameters within which belief is restricted. People and religious communities need to feel empathy with the objects of their faith or cult. This might explain the reason why, despite the express instructions and warnings found in the Koran, Muslims in general have venerated certain individuals and made them holy and almost supernatural. The Prophet Muhammad was the first victim, so to speak, of popularization; he

was made a miracle worker, a magician, and a fortune-teller. Muhammad, despite being entirely human, is popularly considered a kind of supersaint and adored in all times and places through the observance of his ways (Sunna –"the custom") which permeate home and family.

Muhammad inculcated a sense of brotherhood and a spiritual bond between all Muslims. The presence of Allah, made manifest through the words of the Prophet, makes everyday existence sacred for the individual. In a lesser way, the presence of a particularly holy being sanctifies a place or a mosque. Again, despite the official line, Muslims have been known to worship at the tombs of saints,

RABE'A AL-ADAWIYA

Rabe'a al-Adawiya was born in humble circumstances and sold into slavery as a child. She later settled in Basra where she attained great fame as a saint and a preacher. Legend tells that the night Rabe'a came to earth, there was nothing to eat in her father's house for he was very poor. There was no lamp, no oil to rub on her tiny body, and no rug to wrap her in. He already had three daughters and he called the lastborn Rabe'a, meaning "the fourth."

His wife begged him to go to his neighbors and ask them for a drop of oil to light the lamp. The father, however, had made a vow never to ask a mortal being for anything, so he just laid his hand on the neighbor's door and returned. "They will not open the door," he told his wife. She cried bitterly and the man, feeling devastated, placed his head on his knees and went to sleep. He dreamed that he saw the Prophet who told him not be sorrowful, for the girl who had just come to earth was to become a queen among women and his intercessor in the community. The Prophet also instructed him to go to the governor of Basra the next morning and hand him a piece of paper upon which God had instructed the governor to send him one hundred blessings every night and four hundred on Friday. Because the governor had forgotten the blessings on the previous Friday he now had to pay the man four hundred dinars. Rabe'a's father burst into tears upon waking, wrote God's instructions on a piece of paper and promptly went to the governor. When he saw the missive, the governor commanded that he be given two thousand dinars and that he let him know of anything else he might need. Rabe'a's father accepted the money and provided for his family.

When Rabe'a was a little older, and her mother and father had died, a great famine afflicted Basra and she and her sisters were scattered to different places. An evil man seized her and sold her into slavery for six dirhams. Her master put her to hard labor. Rabe'a fasted and served God by day and at night she worshipped standing until dawn. One night the master woke up and saw her praying; he saw that there was a lantern miraculously suspended above her head, the light of which filled the whole house. Frightened, he decided to give Rabe'a her freedom. She went to the desert where she lived in a hermitage and served God.

However, she was determined to go on pilgrimage to Mecca and packed her belongings on the back of a donkey. While journeying through the desert, the donkey died and Rabe'a was left alone. She was praying to God for assistance when she saw the donkey stir and get up again, and so she resumed the pilgrimage. Rabe'a, by her example, introduced the concept of Divine Love into Islamic mysticism.

The beautifully crafted window of an Indian mosque offers a resting place for two doves.

where they derive both blessings and comfort for the distress of daily existence.

It is perhaps ironic that a noteworthy opponent of the emerging cult of saints – a famous scholar named Ibn Taimiya, who lived in the thirteenth and fourteenth centuries – came to be regarded as a saint himself after his death. During his life he had done much to put strong emphasis on the bounty which had already been bestowed upon mankind by God, declaring that to worship saints was to deny the

truth of Islam. So great was his fame that two hundred thousand men reputedly participated at his funeral. His tomb, moreover, was visited by admirers who sought his blessings and attempted to emulate his power of faith.

Perhaps the most famous Islamic "saint" is Sayyid Ahmad al-Badawi, whose complex is in the city of Tanta in the Egyptian delta. "Sidi Ahmad" (meaning Saint Ahmad), as he is popularly called, was born in Fez, Morocco, in about the year 1200 CE, of parents

Below: *Illustration to a sixteenth-century biography of a Sufi shaikh, showing musicians and dancers in a courtyard. Music and dance are a Sufi means of attaining transcendence. A Sufi is a mystic whose goal is to strengthen his or her faith and then transcend it by gaining the love and certainty which spring from direct knowledge of God. Opposite: Moorish stained glass window in Portugal. The sublime patterns of Islamic art sought to reflect the perfection of an all-pervasive deity.*

who were reputedly descended from Ali, the son-in-law of the Prophet. Ahmad was taken to Mecca while he was still a small boy and remained there to complete his studies. When he was about thirty years of age, he underwent a deep spiritual crisis which resulted in a dramatic transformation. He became a mystic, withdrew from society, and concentrated on spiritual exercises, often falling into deep trances. He visited the tombs of famous saints with his brother. He received a vision that called him to travel to Tanta in Egypt where he remained until his death in 1237 CE. It is reported that while in Tanta he spent long periods on the rooftop of his house, staring at the sun until his eyes became inflamed, and fasting for long periods. Supposedly twelve disciples joined him and also lived on the roof in similarly austere conditions.

In many ways Sidi Ahmad is the single most important saint of Islam and his festival, held every autumn, draws more than a million pilgrims each year, almost rivaling the pilgrimage to Mecca.

THE SUFI SAINTS

At the heart of Islam there exists a mystical current called Sufism, whose literature and culture are of extraordinary beauty, bringing alive Islamic spirituality. A Sufi is a Muslim whose goal is to strengthen his or her faith and then transcend it by gaining the love and certainty which spring from direct knowledge of God. The main goal of Sufism is the spiritual union of the individual with God, and as such it represents a path of initiation into spiritual self-purification and self-realization. The Sufi adept passes through various stages of perfection whereby he or she acquires particular virtues or powers. Invocation or prayers open the heart to celestial influences and to the world beyond the senses, or the realm of God. It is within the mysticism of Sufism that we find the greatest saints of Islam.

Apart from Sufi saints, Islam has produced other holy beings at the periphery of mainstream belief. Traditionally Morocco, for instance, presents a form

Opposite: *A painting portraying a Sufi saint meditating deep in nature.* Below: *The vitality of Sufi art. The main goal of Sufism is the spiritual union of the soul with God, a yearning often described in Sufi poetry as a burning flame within one's heart.*

العُلَماء وَرَثَةُ الأنبياء

قالَ رَسُولُ اللَّهَ : إِنَّ

Above: *The Holy Prophet has said: "Verily the men of knowledge are the inheritors of the prophets."* Left: *Mountain fort and walled village near Tafroute, Atlas Mountains, Morocco.*

of sainthood which is linked to holy warfare; these saints are the "marabouts" who were reputedly blessed and had a special link with God. They were members of a Muslim religious community housed in a fortified monastery. Among their numbers were men who possessed certain religious qualifications, such as the reciters of the Koran, transmitters of the Hadith, jurists of Islamic law, and ascetics, and they were held in high esteem by the local community. The marabouts have given their name to one of the most eminent medieval dynasties, the Almoravids. The marabout was believed to be a saint either because of proof of miracles, or because of direct descent from the Prophet as "sharif." After a marabout's death, his sacred power continued to work at his tomb or through his descendants, some of whom might in their turn be regarded as saints.

Marabouts have been attributed the power to heal, to divine, and to intercede with God on behalf of mankind. They were also supposedly capable of bringing rain, flying about, becoming invisible, or changing shape. Because marabouts could be dangerous as well as beneficial, it was necessary for the faithful to propitiate them.

Below: *"Salah" – devotional worship at the Madwah Prophet's Mosque, Juma'a, Saudi Arabia.* Opposite: *A winged angel. It is thought that God has appointed saints as the governors of the universe.*

Proper worship of Allah is measured in degrees of perfection realizable by attaining certain qualities of character and spirit. As a consequence there exists a recognizable hierarchy of sainthood believed to have been set up by God for the benefit of mankind. It is thought that God has appointed saints as the governors of the universe, and they come to earth entirely devoted to his will. They have ceased to follow sensual perceptions. Through their blessing rain falls from heaven; through the purity of their lives, plants grow upon the soil; and through their spiritual influence Muslims gain victories over the Infidels.

There also exists a belief that four thousand saints are hidden from humankind and do not know either one another or their enlightened state. Additionally, there is a special group of 355 who constitute God's court and who are arranged in a hierarchical order. At the highest level of this special group there is one exceptional saint called the "Pole," who exists at the center of the cosmos, around which everything revolves and from which the created order draws its energy and form. Apparently the Pole assumes the identity of a different individual in each age; even though they are believed to be the highest form of being apart from God, the Poles are disguised as real persons who engage in ordinary human activities, and they are only known by those who are spiritually aware. Their true identities, however, cannot be revealed to others.

It is popularly believed that walis are chosen by God and that no amount of pious behavior will bring this quality to anyone; this state is described

as a "rapture" or a "captivation" with the divine, as though these individuals were "drunk" with God. This state, however, may not always appear as saintly in the sense of good and pious; walis can behave in very bizarre ways, drawing a fine line between madness and sainthood. In order to prevent the faithful from admiring and perhaps even worshipping individuals who are mad, there are certain rules which help one distinguish the true saint from the true fool. The saint who behaves in a crazed manner can be recognized by the fact that he or she possesses a rational soul which is intact, and that there exists a deep devotion and constant divine worship, although perhaps not according to the parameters defined in religious law. The soul of a truly foolish person, on the other hand, is corrupt and he or she may worship anything, without discrimination.

The duty of all Muslims is to bind themselves to the command of Allah and to express their commitment to him in prayer and in everyday acts. Thus to be a saint, in Muslim terms, means to absorb the will of Allah into one's own being to such an extent as to be completely transformed by love and light. One's being is placed at the mercy of Allah and one's life is lived for the exaltation of his name.

Below: *A sadhu bearing the colored marks of the god Vishnu on his forehead.*
Opposite, top: *The interior of the temple contains a Shiva lingam where the faithful*
make offerings. Bottom: *Daily ritual bathing in the river Ganges.*

CHAPTER FIVE

THE HINDU PATH TO SAINTHOOD

hen traveling through India the visitor is struck by the myriad living symbols of devotion to be found everywhere: temples, lingams, yonis, sacred cows, burning incense, sadhus, priestly Brahmins, market stalls replete with prayer mats, prayer bells, prayer shawls; devotees practicing purification rites by a river, the dead on funeral pyres at the burning grounds. There are innumerable religious ceremonies, observances, fasts, feasts, pilgrimages. Everywhere one looks there is a living expression of devotion – to a god, to a goddess, to the higher self. This is the main reason why the land of India has fascinated the world for centuries.

This outward expression of spirituality is, however, not restricted to mere ritual. Hinduism, one of the three major religions of the sub-continent (the other two being Buddhism and Jainism), has over the centuries deeply influenced both the structure of Hindu society and the individual psyche. All Hindus are expected, through a process of many lifetimes, to finally leave "samsara" (the cycle of death and rebirth) and to attain "moksha" (liberation). Those who embark upon the path towards final liberation are considered holy by all Hindus, for they possess the clarity of vision that leads them to the destiny which ultimately belongs to all. To be a Hindu, in other words, means to be traveling somewhere on the long path to sainthood.

Below: *A small altar with flowers placed in offering.* Opposite: *The epic hero Rama, his beautiful wife Sita, and Hanuman, the monkey god. The seventh incarnation of the god Vishnu, sustainer of the universe, Rama remains for comtemporary India the perfect model of humanity.*

ATTAINING HOLINESS: BREAKING THE LAW OF KARMA

Hindu doctrine teaches the principle of the transmigration of the soul from life to life, and hands down a corollary belief in "karma," or the collection of previous acts which determine the form into which one is to be reborn. Any earthly process, in this context, is viewed as cyclical and all worldly existence is subject to this cycle. Samsara thus has no beginning and, in most cases, no end. And karma binds the souls of all beings to the world and compels them to go through an endless series of deaths and rebirths. The *raison d'être* of every soul is to attain final liberation either in this life, if one has perfected oneself in previous existences, or in some future life. Sainthood

is thus not perceived as an impossible ideal, or a gift given to the chosen few by God, but as an inevitable conclusion of the process of karma.

India, more than any other land, has given birth to innumerable saints; some were ordinary individuals who achieved enlightenment under the guidance of gurus, others were inspired directly by a god or goddess. The phenomenon of saints underscores the Hindu belief that everyone is able to reach these heights of consciousness. When a saint dies in India, he or she is not burned on the pyre like all others, but the body is kept in a special crypt, called a "samadhi," so that the healing energy emanating from it can go on radiating for years. The radiation emitted by a saint is believed to be a powerful trigger which awakens the spirit within other people.

Opposite: *A potter fashioning candle-burning pots to be used at a religious festival. Right: Mounds of red powder on sale at a market stall – the powder is used by women to make the tikha mark borne on the third eye as a sign of divine aid.*

The recognition of the divine potential which is latent in all humans finds symmetry, and is further explicated, in the anthropomorphism of the Hindu pantheon. The main deities display human characteristics; they are male and female, they love and hate each other, and are enraged by humans. The Hindu belief is that a deity who displays human characteristics can fully understand the human condition. Not only that, there is an ascending movement in the religious mode that accepts "highly evolved" individuals as manifesting the divine nature in a particularly vivid way. So, not only are Hindu gods human but humans can be, and are expected to be, gods – these are the saints of Hinduism.

These two very ancient precepts find manifestation in many of the socio-religious orders that bind the extensive Hindu community. The social structure, and this is a vivid example, is divided into four religious castes: Brahmins, Ksatriyas, Vaisyas, and Sudras.

The Brahmins claim, whatever their worldly occupation, to be by virtue of their birth a perpetual incarnation of the "dharma" (the supreme doctrine), and to be the guardians and dispensers of divine power. They are entitled to teach the Veda (sacred scriptures), to perform religious ceremonies and sacrifices for others, and to receive gifts and alms. Brahmins are held to be the highest of all human beings and it is believed that the divine actually inhabits their caste. It is

interesting to note that Hinduism believes in the divine quality of the leadership of the social hierarchy. The nobility, the Ksatriyas, are the protectors of the people; the duty of the commoners, the Vaisyas, is to raise cattle, to trade, and to cultivate the land. Finally, the untouchables, the Sudras, traditionally have the duty "to serve" and thus are charged with impure occupations such as sweeping or carrying corpses. The Sudras often have no home and live and die in the streets in conditions of extreme poverty.

It could be argued that the caste system represents a precise framework for the soul to evolve: the principles that rule the system are so strict that they force spiritual evolution. Upon rebirth the soul "knows" – because the system allows that knowledge – what caste to reincarnate into, so that whatever has been learned in the previous existence can be put to best use in this life.

This social system goes hand in hand with the principles of karma and samsara – there exists a correspondence between the social system and the religious hells and heavens, and the social system is the framework within which karma works in this world. If one has practiced asceticism and lived according to religious principles, then the soul is bound to reincarnate in a Brahmin body. If, on the other hand, one has accumulated sins in a previous life, then this existence will be lived in a low social caste.

Below: *A sadhu wearing a mala around his neck. The beads represent moments in one's existence pierced through by the divine essence (the string of the necklace).* Opposite: *Worshipping at the temple is one of the most important activities of the day for all Hindus. In those moments of silent meditation and prayer, the individual is reminded of the divine essence which inhabits every soul.*

EVERYDAY SAINTS

Because Hinduism is as much a way of life as a religious system, the general characteristics of asceticism and renunciation have been incorporated also into the common psychological outlook. These practices are best exemplified in the manners of upper-caste, middle-class Hindus. This mode has influenced the husband-and-wife and child-parent relationships; there is restraint in the display of emotions, smiles are hoarded, vigorous physical movement like running or dancing is avoided. In public, hand gestures and facial expression while conversing are rare. Human relationships put others at a distance. The tone overall is of a certain detachment, as though the world and its pleasures are only transitory.

Even though this behavior may seem accidental, it hides a deeper meaning: these disciplines are intended to bring the individual under restraint, so that he or she will attain greater calm and be

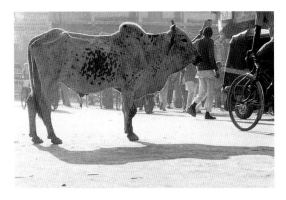

prepared for meditation and the control of the activities of the mind and the desires of the body.

Hinduism has devised a life-order by which everyone can attain final liberation from the law of karma. This order divides life into two: the first half to be lived within society, and the second half to be lived outside social demands. Each half, in turn, is divided into two, the first part of each being a preparation for the second, as follows: first of all as a student, learning the skills and duties of the caste, and practicing obedience; then, as a responsible householder in marriage, fulfilling without question all of the duties of the caste. Mid-life is the time when one may depart from society to seriously undertake the practice of meditation, and finally, achieving liberation, to release the self from the chains of karma. In a sense, therefore, the "sannyasin" – one who departs society for "better" things - is the saint in preparation.

The whole of Hindu society is furthermore subject to strict rules of asceticism which are progressively increased in the ascending order of the social and religious hierarchy. The ideal of "ahimsa," or non-injury, is also cultivated. This is the absence of the desire to harm, manifested in the preference of most Hindus for a vegetarian diet and in the worship of the cow, an animal which gives food without having to be killed. Private rituals include the morning ceremonies of self-purification, bathing, prayers, and recitation of mantras, the offering of water and flowers to the sun, meditative concentration, and evening worship at the temple.

Opposite: *All Hindus practice the ideal of ahimsa, non-injury; this is the desire not to harm, which is manifested in the worship of the cow, an animal which provides nourishment without having to be killed.*
Below: *Ritual bathing in the Ganges, the holy river for all Hindus.*

Below: *Sadhu sitting at his shrine.* Opposite: *A sadhu meditates under a tree, early in the morning.*
Sadhus are ascetics who have left society and devote their lives to raising their consciousness. They are the
holy people of India.

THE WANDERING SADHUS

The Hindu standards of saintliness are realized in thousands upon thousands of holy men and women throughout the land. It is socially acceptable, and widely practiced, for an individual to leave the family after his or her duties have been completed, such as when the children have married or the spouse has died. The person whose worldly and family function has ended is thus ready to embrace the spiritual life and he or she may opt to become a wandering sadhu.

The practice of asceticism is furthered in the religious and mendicant life, for, having shed the worldly self, the person must now raise his or her consciousness to a higher level. Sadhus, for instance, are easily recognizable throughout India: their foreheads are marked by a symbol denoting both their religion and their asceticism. They wear only a loincloth (and sometimes clothing is entirely dispensed with), they smear their bodies with consecratory ashes, dress their hair with cow dung and urine, carry a human skull to show that they are beyond the terror of death,

Below: *Sadhus often submit themselves to extreme forms of yogic exercises and ascetic practices to tame the flesh so that the spirit can blossom.* Bottom: *Female sannyasin.* Opposite: *Two holy men in a forest clearing. Painting from Murshidabad, c. 1760-63.*

and take vows of celibacy. They live with a minimum of possessions, namely a begging bowl and a walking staff, and submit their bodies to extreme forms of yogic exercises to tame the flesh so that the spirit may blossom.

Sadhus are wholly maintained by ordinary people who fill their begging bowls with left-over food, contribute to their welfare, and seek their blessings. Offering charity of this kind to sadhus is considered a holy act insofar as it ultimately karmically rewards the ordinary individual. Thus, all Hindus tolerate and sustain religious ascetics who have abandoned social life in order to concentrate on physical and spiritual discipline.

RAMAKRISHNA

Ramakrishna was one the greatest Hindu saints who demonstrated enlightenment by personal example. He was born in 1836 of a poor Brahmin family, refused to follow any formal education, and only spoke a coarse Bengali dialect throughout his life. At the age of twenty-three he was married to Sarada-devi, who was then aged five; the marriage was never consummated when she grew up because Ramakrishna had taken vows of celibacy. Sarada-devi was later deified and is still considered a saint by the Ramakrishna sect.

Rather than learning about God from books, Ramakrishna wished to realize Him through his everyday acts and worship. He became God-intoxicated at the age of seven when he fell into a mystical trance. When he was older he fought against sexual passion and money, for he believed that they caused men to fail to achieve spiritual enlightenment; his objection to money became so strong that it was said that gold or metal had an allergic effect upon him.

Ramakrishna considered Kali, the Hindu goddess of creation and destruction, to be the supreme manifestation of God. He called her the Divine Mother and worshipped at her temple on the outskirts of Calcutta. There he was said to weep for hours at a time and to feel a burning sensation throughout his body while imploring Kali to reveal herself to him. Visions of Kali eventually brought him great peace and inner stillness.

He embarked upon twelve years of strict ascetic exercises attaining varying degrees of samadhi (the ultimate silence). He took sannyas from a monk named Totapuri, and under his guidance achieved Nirvikalpa samadhi, or final union with the divine. Thousands of people came to hear his discourses at his home in Calcutta which today houses the headquarters of his movement. Ramakrishna saw God in everyone and everything; he claimed that all spiritual paths lead to the same goal.

The Guru:
The Transmission of Light

The concept that characterizes Hinduism, namely that of the perfectibility of mankind, is best exemplified in the relationship between gurus and their disciples. Hindu gurus are the true saints, spiritual guides who have attained full enlightenment through meditation and ascetic practices. These holy beings represent burning lights in the darkness of mass unconsciousness (the word guru literally means one who brings light into darkness) and their chief responsibility is to transmit the light to all others. From ancient times, Hinduism has stressed the fundamental importance of the tutorial method in religious instruction. In the educational system of ancient India, for instance, we find that knowledge of the Vedas was transmitted through oral teachings from the guru to his pupil. The pupil lived at the home of the guru and served him with obedience and devotion. With the rise of the bhakti movement, which stressed devotion to a personified deity, the function of the guru became even more important. He or she not only became the leader and founder of religious sects, but was also considered to be the living embodiment of the spiritual truth, and thus identified with the deity.

This tradition has continued to the present day. India is dotted with ashrams and monastic communities where powerful individuals daily transmit wisdom to their disciples, or sannyasins. Initiation into sannyas is a sort of purification and consecration which indicates the transformation from the worldly self to the spiritual self. Often a devotional name is given to the person to mark this transformation. A period of probation might be required by the guru, consisting of either the study of the holy scriptures or the intense practice of yoga.

In the past three decades, many Westerners have felt attracted to the ascetic life conducted in Indian ashrams. Even though such movements are popularly called "cults" – usually with negative connotations implying exploitation of the individual – gurus and their disciples, whether they be Westerners or

Venkataraman was born in Madurai (near Madras, southern India) in 1879, into a middle-class Brahmin family. He read mysticism and devotional literature, and was captivated by legends of the local place of pilgrimage, Mount Arunachala, from which the God Siva was believed to have arisen in a spiral of fire at the creation of the world.

At the age of seventeen Venkataraman had a spiritual experience whereupon he felt a great fear of death and, lying very still on the floor, he imagined his body becoming a cold, stiff corpse. From this experience he derived his technique of self-inquiry ("vicara"). Through a path of progressive negation, he began inquiring into the substance of the self; to the question "Who am I?" he answered, "Not the body, because it is decaying; not the mind, because the brain will decay with the body; not the personality, nor the emotions, because these will vanish with death." His intense desire to experience the essence of the self brought him to a state of pure consciousness and bliss, to "samadhi." He thus abandoned all his possessions, shaved his head, and became a hermit on Mount Arunachala where he took the name of Ramana Maharshi. He was one of the most famous and influential gurus of India and thousands of seekers visited him in order to learn how to practice vicara.

Opposite: *Sathya Sai Baba sits in meditation.*
Above: *Ramana Maharshi.*

Indians, generally fit into the traditional background of Hindu spirituality. In this sense they are not innovative, and their appeal may lie exactly in the fact that they represent an established format within which the individual can deepen his or her interest in spiritual liberation, albeit outside standard society. The denigration of modern cults by the West thus denotes a lack of understanding of the religious traditions of the East.

Opposite: *Krishna with companions in the moonlight.* Below: *The divine union of male and female seen here in a sculpture in the Ellora temple of South India.*

THE BHAKTI SAINTS

Hinduism has produced myriad saints and holy people who represent the paradigm of religiousness for the laity in everyday life. Certain saints have, however, signified in a particularly vivid way their devotion to a different kind of reality. Among them, there are the saints belonging to the medieval Bhakti movement, developed throughout India around the sixth century CE.

The Bhakti movement centers on the devotion to Lord Krishna, expressed in mystical poetry and song, chanted in the common languages of the people and not in Sanskrit (the language of the holy scriptures). The relationship between the worshipper and the divinity can best be described as being that between lover and beloved; the object of meditation is the Lord Krishna and love is the medium within which the soul is spiritually elevated. The most famous collection of Bhakti poems and songs is the Bhaktamal, or "Garland of Devotees," which is a record of the lives and virtues of these saints.

The mystical poetess Mira Bai is one the most famous, and she is greatly loved by popular Hindu culture; songs attributed to her are sung from one end of the subcontinent to the other, and many feature-length movies have been produced about her life and her deeds. She reputedly was a Rajput princess so absorbed in her love of the Lord Krishna that she saw herself as his bride, and from childhood displayed a lack of interest in her worldly role. Her family betrothed her to a man from the nobility, but

Opposite: *The Lord Krishna, the most charming of the incarnations of the god Vishnu, who inspired the powerful movement of the Bhakti saints.*

when she recited the mantras during her wedding, she directed her devotion not to her husband but to Lord Krishna instead. Instead of the traditional dowry, she asked for an image of Krishna. When she arrived at her husband's house, Mira Bai refused to bow her head to her mother-in-law or to the chosen goddess of the house as was customary. This defiance incensed her husband and her parents-in-law, for it cast discredit on the new family and on her own lineage as well.

Mira's conviction that she had already offered herself to the Lord Krishna threatened the status quo. Instead of the new family of her husband, she embraced the family of the saints – the sadhus and wandering mendicants who worshipped Krishna. She fed them, listened to them, and admired their principles. In this sense, Mira Bai was no different from the gopis, the legendary earthly wives of Krishna who, although married, abandoned the conventional morality of their day and ran to Krishna whenever he played his flute. They left their brooms and cooking implements, they even leapt out of the marital bed, to go and dance in the forests with their beloved God.

Mira Bai's husband was so annoyed by the conduct of his wife that he prepared a cup of poison in the guise of an offering to the Lord Krishna, knowing that Mira would eat and drink anything that was left over from the God's table. However, when she drank the poison the liquid turned into sweet ambrosia, as though she had really tasted a heavenly drink. Soon there were rumors that Mira had other men, and her husband, more incensed than ever, turned his murderous attentions towards these mysterious lovers. Finally when someone heard Mira Bai talking sweetly in her chambers, the husband was summoned and he appeared, sword in hand ready to kill. But when he demanded to see the man she was talking to, Mira responded that it was Krishna, her beloved Lord, and that he would not shy away from a fight. At that point, according to the story, the husband fled in terror – the flesh and blood husband turned to stone in his terror, while the image was more alive than him, for it was the image of a God.

Mira Bai proved her fearlessness in another episode of her life when she traveled to Brindavan, the site of one of the most important temples to Krishna. Because she was a woman, she was refused an audience with a great philosopher who resided within the walls. Mira Bai taught him a lesson when she sent him a message stating that in Brindavan there was only one male, the Lord Krishna, and all true male devotees were like women in their worship of the Lord. The philosopher acknowledged her wisdom, agreed to give her an audience, and thanked her for displaying to him the depth of her devotion.

The religious message of Mira Bai is that devotion in Bhakti expression has threatening consequences for ordinary morality; the Bhakti saints, in other words, incarnate a living morality which is more genuine than that taught in the holy scriptures.

MAHATMA GANDHI

Mohandas Karamchand Gandhi was a small man whose great message appealed to the hearts of the Indian people as no other had, possibly since the days of the Buddha. By the strength of his principles and moral power he shook the British Empire to its very foundations, and was able to promote great social change by evoking the natural goodness of mankind. The word *mahatma* means "great soul" and the title was first given to Gandhi by Rabindranath Tagore, the Indian poet, when Gandhi arrived in India from South Africa in 1915.

Even though Gandhi is not strictly venerated as a religious saint, in the sense that he is not a household manifestation of divine power to which candles are lit and offerings made daily, he nevertheless is venerated for provoking social change through his own practices of asceticism. His doctrine of non-violence, derived from Hindu sources, was one of the most striking characteristics of his ideology. The austere and celibate life that he imposed upon himself, his family, and the inhabitants of his ashrams, further proved his role as a quintessential representation of the Hindu tradition.

Although he was a man among men, Gandhi nevertheless possessed the characteristics that heroes and saints are made of: he demonstrated the political power of love and, like the Christian ascetics, was ready to undergo the severest trials in order to prove the sincerity of his beliefs. He helped Indians to see a way through to social justice and political independence, as well as inspiring them to moral and spiritual heights.

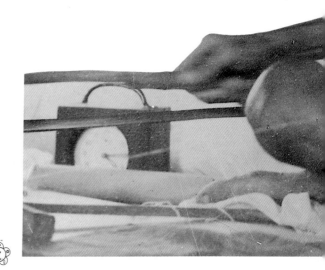

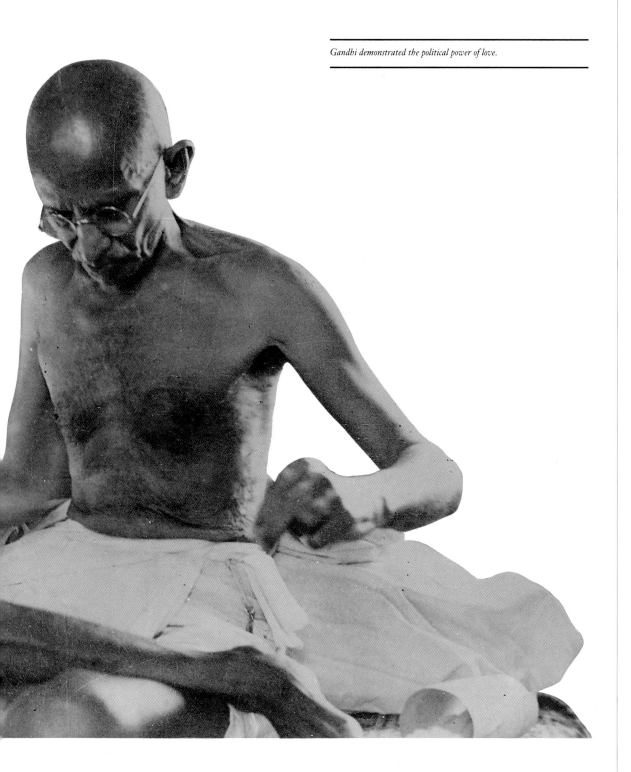

Gandhi demonstrated the political power of love.

Below: *The Buddha, wearing the robes of a fully ordained monk, sits in the lotus pose, and from his golden colored body light rays emanate, reaching out to all sentient beings and fulfilling all their wishes.* Opposite: *Buddhist monks sit in meditation.*

CHAPTER SIX

THE BUDDHIST PARADIGMS OF MAN PERFECTED

"Buddham saranam gacchami
Dhammam saranam gacchami
Sangham saranam gacchami."

"To the Buddha [the Enlightened Teacher]
for Refuge I go,
To the Dharma [the Way to Enlightenment]
for Refuge I go,
To the Sangha [the spiritual community of those
who walk the Way to Enlightenment]
or Refuge I go."

his chant represents the absolute spiritual commitment of a seeker to the Three Jewels of Buddhism – the Buddha, the Dharma, and the Sangha – and "taking refuge," in this sense, means to place this commitment at the center of life, discarding all other worldly involvements, in order to seek perfection. If the individual state of religiousness can be defined as the achievement of psychological and spiritual wholeness, then Buddhism, in its 2,500 years of history, has carved the way to that wholeness. Buddhism is the way to enlightenment, and within the Buddhist tradition the only form of sainthood that can exist is that of enlightenment.

The Dharma, as taught by the Buddha after his experience of enlightenment, follows very precise steps to the attainment of Nirvana, the ultimate freedom, wisdom, and compassion. These steps can best be followed within a spiritual community, the Sangha, of those committed to the attainment of the same experience, helping each other along the path. Despite forming the basis for one of the most ancient religions, the message of the Buddha remains contemporary and seems to appeal more and more to the modern mind.

It is the centrality of the individual experience, rather than adherence to religious ideals, that forms the paradigm of individual sainthood within Buddhism. The Buddha carved a path that everyone is invited to follow – the path that leads to ultimate perfection and holiness.

THE BUDDHA

The word Buddha is not in fact a name at all, but rather a title meaning "The Awakened One," or the "One Who Knows, One Who Understands" – one who, in other words, has awakened to the Ultimate Reality. The first bearer of this title was a man called Gautama Siddhartha, who lived in the sixth century BCE in the area which is now partly modern Nepal, partly northern India.

Gautama Siddhartha was born into a patrician family and received a high level of education. When he was sixteen years of age, his family arranged for him to marry a cousin and a few years later a son was born. Despite his wealth and the fact that he led what might seem to us a very easy existence, historical accounts point to a certain dissatisfaction with life which led him to a deep spiritual crisis, the turning point in his life. The crisis began when he saw the "Four Sights," which represented a spiritual awakening, the impact of which is central to Buddhist teaching.

Legend tells that one beautiful morning Siddhartha decided to go out for a ride in his chariot, in the company of his charioteer. On reaching the local town, Siddhartha saw his "First Sight"– an old man. According to the legend he had never seen an old person before.

Opposite: *The temptations of the Buddha – these were thought to be demons that the Buddha fought during his meditations to gain enlightenment.* Below: *A Tibetan tangka portraying a Bodhisattva.*

The "Second Sight" was of sickness; he realized that all human beings, even though they might be strong and healthy as he was, might one day be struck down by maladies without warning.

The "Third Sight" was a corpse being carried to the burning grounds on a stretcher. Siddartha saw that there were certain things over which there was no control – one was bound to grow old, one could be struck by sickness, and death was an absolute certainty looming ahead. This posed an existential riddle, a mystery he wished to find answers for.

The "Fourth Sight" was of a sadhu, or holy man, walking through the streets with his begging bowl. Despite his poverty, this man seemed to Siddhartha to be calm and peaceful, a state that seemed highly enviable. The youth considered that if he were to abandon all his riches and don saffron robes like those worn by the sadhu, he might find the answer to the questions tormenting him, so he became a homeless wanderer in search of the truth.

Siddhartha practiced the most severe of austerities, as was the custom in India among sadhus. However, even though he became a great ascetic and gathered a few disciples around him, he saw that this form of self-torture was not leading him towards the truth, and subsequently decided to give it up. When he began to eat again, his disciples left him in disgust. The story goes that once, alone and on his travels, he came to a beautiful spot by the banks of a flowing river, and there made the resolution to sit and not rise again until he had reached enlightenment.

Left: *The podium at Sarnath, where the Buddha gave his first discourse after his enlightenment.* Below: *A very young Buddhist scholar sits in the morning mists outside the temple.*

Day after day, night after night, he remained. Controlling and concentrating his mind, purifying his spirit, he overcame mental hindrances and on Wesak night, the night of the full moon in May, just as the morning star was rising, he attained full enlightenment.

Siddhartha, who had now become the Buddha, had attained what he had wished for during so many years. He gathered the disciples who had left him and started to spread his teaching. He taught everyone – men and women, princes and beggars, wealthy landowners and poor peasants. When he died, in his eightieth year, thousands of ordinary people and disciples mourned his departure.

The significance of this story is central to Buddhism insofar as Gautama Siddhartha was an ordinary human being who, through his own efforts and concentration, attained the Supreme Reality. The Buddha is not a god, he is an ordinary human being who becomes enlightened. And such a being, or Buddha, is, according to Buddhist tradition, the highest being in the universe, higher even than the so-called gods. Throughout Buddhist art the gods are represented in humble positions on either side of the Buddha, saluting him, paying homage, and listening to his teaching.

The Buddha returned to the world of men to teach them awakening. Buddhas are thus "awakeners," rousing every man and woman who wishes to be awakened in order to rise from the clouds of illusion and tread the Way to enlightenment.

THE ARAHANT

According to the Buddhist belief system there are
four types of holy individuals who span the gap
between Buddhahood and ordinary, unenlightened
humanity. These are: the Stream-Entrant, the Once-
Returner, the Non-Returner, and the Arahant. These
four types of holy individuals are distinguished from
one another by the degree of their insight into the
nature of reality. Buddhists measure holiness by the
intensity experienced in deep meditation which
allows the individual to see the illusion of wordly
concepts and ideas. The greater the experience, the
more piercing the insight, the more concepts are seen
as mere illusions and thus abandoned. These
illusionary concepts are regarded as fetters which
chain the soul to the Wheel of Karma and thus
prevent the individual from attaining final liberation,
and therefore, in effect, "sainthood."

The first holy person – the Stream-Entrant (Pali
srotapanna, which literally means "one who has
entered the stream of higher consciousness") – has
seen the illusion of death, the hindrance to
spirituality represented by doubts and indecisions,

Below: *A temple wall portraying Bodhisattvas who have come to bring light into the world.* Opposite: *Arahants, having attained perfect enlightenment, vibrate in unison with the world.*

and the attachment to rites and ceremonies. Buddhist doctrine teaches that once someone has become a Stream-Entrant, then he or she will only have to return for another seven lives before attaining enlightenment.

The second holy person, a step higher than the Stream-Entrant, is the Once-Returner (Pali "sakrdagamin") – the person who returns only once more to this earth as a human being. This individual has understood the need to abandon all desire for sensuous existence and anger, but has not transcended them yet.

The Non-Returner (Pali "anagamin"), who will no longer need to return to earth as a human being, has transcended all anger and the need for sensuous existence.

The fourth holy person is the Arahant, meaning "the worthy." The Arahant's depth of meditation is so powerful as to break all chains that bind him to the Wheel of Karma. The Arahant is worshipped in all Buddhist circles as a saint – one, in other words, who through his own concentration and depth of meditation has attained the Buddha-nature. In breaking the chains that bind him to the Wheel of Karma, the Arahant also develops what are known as the six powers which are believed to be the gifts of his deep meditation:

1. Psycho-kinetic activity – these are miraculous deeds. For example, the Arahant may become invisible, travel through air, walk on water, travel to the moon.

2. Divine ear – the power to hear any sounds in heaven or on earth.

3. The power to penetrate and discern the minds of others.

4. Knowledge of previous existences.

5. Divine eye – clairvoyance and the full understanding of karmic law.

6. Knowledge of the destruction of the asravas, the mental poisons that flood the mind.

SARIPUTTA

Sariputta was one of the leading disciples of Sanjaya, a prominent scholar and philosopher. Early one morning, while Sariputta was walking through the streets of his town, Rajagaha, he came upon a mendicant monk who was begging for food. He was so impressed by the propriety of the monk that he decided to follow him. When he asked the monk who he was, the humble man replied that he had abandoned secular life to follow the teaching of the Buddha and that the Buddha had explained the law of causation and how it could be broken to attain final liberation. Sariputta decided that this was the teaching that he had sought for so long, but had not found with his teacher Sanjaya. He thus followed the monk to the Bamboo Grove Monastery and there met the Buddha who told him that he would become a great jewel, shining supreme among his disciples. Sariputta, having placed his faith in the Buddha, attained perfect enlightenment, and became a model of humbleness and self-discipline for all the disciples of all times.

MOGALLANA

Mogallana was a friend of Sariputta's and had studied with him under the teacher Sanjaya. It was Sariputta who convinced Mogallana to leave all behind and to follow the teaching of the Buddha, and just as his friend achieved foremost wisdom, Mogallana acquired complete freedom in supernatural powers at the Jetavana Monastery. Here he decided to use his supernatural powers to discover where his deceased mother had been reborn and to try and recompense her for the care she had given him as a child. After many inquiries he discovered that she was suffering in the hell of hungry demons. He thus used his powers to send her a bowl of food. She was overjoyed, but when she tried to put the food in her mouth it burst into flames, causing her even more pain. Greatly grieved by her plight, Mogallana asked the Buddha to save his mother from hell. The Master, however, said that Mogallana's supernatural powers could not help her atone for her sins, and that he should ask the other monks to pray for her – their prayers would free her.

Mogallana became famous for his ability to see what others could not see, hear things others could not hear, read people's minds, read their pasts, and act with perfect freedom.

In order to attain a deep state of concentration, Mogallana left the Bamboo Grove Monastery and went to the nearby Vulture park, where he sat in a cave submitting himself to the strictest disciplines. During the training, he refused to allow himself to sleep or to even rest. When he became discouraged, the Buddha would appear before him and encourage him to persevere. On one occasion Mogallana went to a village to preach, but was so exhausted that he fell asleep. Buddha appeared before him and told him to recite the dharma. When the hard discipline finally brought Mogallana to enlightenment he said, "I have been enlightened because of my master's teaching and encouragement. I have, therefore, been born of my master."

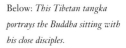

Below: *This Tibetan tangka portrays the Buddha sitting with his close disciples.*

Opposite: *Buddhas carved in stone. Buddhas are "awakeners," rousing every man and woman who wishes to be awakened to rise from the clouds of illusion and tread the Way to enlightenment.*

Subha

Subha was very beautiful and had been born into a wealthy Brahmin family, but she left her world to embrace the ascetic life as a Buddhist nun. While seeking enlightenment she encountered a man in the forest who wished to seduce her. She inquired of him what he found attractive in a body that she now regarded as foul and impermanent. He replied that her doe-eyes inflamed his passion. Subha thus cut out one of her eyes and gave it to him. When she went to the Buddha, he restored her eye and she gained enlightenment.

Opposite: *A tree becomes a place of devotion where people sit in meditation.*
Below: *The bodhi tree in Bodh Gaya, in central Bihar state, northern India, where the Buddha attained his enlightenment.*

ANANDA

Ananda served the Buddha for years as a personal attendant, never leaving his side. Because he had so many opportunities to hear the Buddha speak, and because he both understood and recalled what the Master said perfectly, Ananda was known for hearing the most teachings. Ananda was by nature gentle and sympathetic and found breaking with the delusions of the world very difficult. Aware of his immaturity in spiritual training, he resolved to be discreet, avoid pride, and never stray from the true path. The Buddha chose him as his attendant because of these virtues. When the Master was very old Ananda realized that his death was near and he started to cry bitterly. But the Buddha said to him, "Do not grieve. Although I disappear from this world, I live forever. Follow my instructions, keep the teachings and the precepts diligently, and find perfect enlightenment as soon as possible." Ananda took his Master's counsel to heart and as a result of his diligence he finally attained enlightenment after the Buddha's death. He performed a key service by reciting all the teachings he had heard from the Buddha, enabling others to write them down for the benefit of humanity.

MAHAKASHYAPA

One day, the Buddha was engaged at the Mount of the Holy Vulture in preaching to a large gathering. He sat upon the podium completely silent for a long time, and instead of resorting to a lengthy discourse to explain his point, on that day he lifted a single lotus flower and held it high for everyone to see. No one understood the meaning of this gesture except for the venerable Mahakashyapa, one of the Buddha's disciples, who quietly smiled at the Master, as if fully comprehending the meaning of his silent teaching. The Buddha, perceiving the smile, declared, "I have the most precious treasure, spiritual and transcendental, which this moment I hand over to you, O venerable Mahakashyapa!"

By raising the flower Buddha symbolically revealed the innermost mind of the enlightened one. Mahakashyapa understood the deep significance of this message by letting the silence of the Master penetrate the very depth of his being.

The story of Mahakashyapa is one of the most significant in the teachings of the Buddha. Zen followers trace the birth of the understanding which was eventually to become Zen Buddhism to this moment. Zen teaches sudden enlightenment which is symbolized by the sudden awakening to the truth experienced by Mahakashyapa in the presence of the Buddha. It was as though a thunderbolt had suddenly hit him, breaking the sleep of thousands of years. In that awakening Mahakashyapa knew the mystery of existence.

The first Arahants mentioned in Buddhist scriptures are the close disciples of the Buddha, both men and women, who, we are told, perfected themselves over previous lifetimes and gained enlightenment by either meeting the Buddha or listening to his teaching of the dharma. The meeting with the Master was the key that put an end to all further "becoming" and turned them into "wise-beings" who would not return to life again. Many of these disciples had been born wealthy and, upon meeting the Buddha, had abandoned all their riches and become wandering beggars. Others attained enlightenment by rigorous practice of meditation and asceticism. Free from the snares of desire, they lived in the world, but were not of it.

The close disciples of the Buddha were not just silent, self-centered ascetics. Many, such as Sariputta, employed their wisdom to liberate humanity from its predicament. The Buddha forbade them to use their miraculous powers among the laity to gather disciples – their teaching was to be based solely upon their wisdom and clarity.

All of them have embarked upon the long journey outlined by the deeds and experience of the Buddha. The Arahant, one of two pinnacles of Buddhist

---

Opposite: *A stone carving of the bull, the animal most often used as a symbol of the base nature in Chinese Buddhist stories.* Below: *Forest monks in Burma.*

sainthood, represents the blossoming of the self, the one who attains Buddha-nature by having followed the path set out by the Master.

Today, the paradigm of sainthood represented by the Arahant is still very much a model for Buddhist monks and nuns. The virtues pertaining to the state of the Arahant are cultivated in the enclosure of monasteries, where adepts can focus all their energies toward breaking all the fetters that chain them to the Wheel of Karma. In Thailand, for example, there are forest monks acclaimed as Arahants who reputedly possess great charismatic powers and are visited by the laity for the blessing of amulets. These forest monks live according to strict ascetic disciplines: they use rags and discarded cloth for their robes and they only eat food that has been given to them as alms. Irrespective of wealth and status, they beg from every house; they receive food in their begging bowls and live in forests rather than human settlements. They sit in contemplation in cemeteries and burning grounds in order to understand and free themselves from the processes of growth, decay, death, and rebirth.

Moreover, all the senses are under strict control; wishes are few, and social intercourse is strictly limited. Traditionally, these monks follow the wandering pattern of the Buddha. They travel from village to village for nine months of the year, and for the three monsoon months they reside in one place and teach the Dharma.

THE BODHISATTVA

"For you must know, beloved, that each one of us is beyond all question responsible for all men and all things on earth, not only because of the individual transgression of the world, but each one individually for all men and every single man on this earth. This realization is the crown of a monk's way of life, and, indeed of every man on earth. For a monk is not a different kind of man, but merely such as all men on earth ought to be." (Father Zossima in *The Brothers Karamazov*)

The word Bodhisattva is composed of "bodhi," meaning "the state of being awake" and "sattva,"

meaning "mind" or "intention." Bodhisattva thus means one whose mind or intention is directed towards enlightenment. The ideal of the Bodhisattva arose out of Mahayana Buddhism (in about the eighth century) as a new paradigm of sainthood. It is different from that represented by the Arahant insofar as the Bodhisattva achieves enlightenment by taking upon himself the responsibility of freeing all beings in the universe from suffering and leading them to Nirvana. The Bodhisattva has only two goals in mind: his own attainment of enlightenment and the welfare of all beings, the latter being his main objective.

VIMALKIRTY

Vimalkirty wore the white clothes of an ordinary householder, yet lived a very religious life. Although he lived at home, he is said to have remained detached from desire. He had a son, a wife, and several female attendants with whom he always behaved with restraint and appeared to live as though in utter solitude. He ate and drank but only from a state of meditation. He participated in social events and yet did so in order to bring light to others. He conversed with teachers of other religious traditions, but remained always faithful to the Buddha.

Opposite: *An old Tibetan man sitting outside a temple, reciting mantras with his prayer beads.* Above: *Tibetan monks in a religious procession.* Right: *A Chinese portrait of Vimalkirti, the most famous Indian Bodhisattva.*

There are eight qualifications which must be met by the individual during the life in which he makes a vow to become a Bodhisattva. These are:

1. He must be a human.
2. He must be a male.
3. He must be able to achieve liberation in that lifetime.
4. He must make the vow to become a Bodhisattva in the presence of a living Buddha.
5. He must be a renunciate.
6. He must possess the five powers and the eight attainments. The five powers are: the power to perform physical miracles – such as the ability to appear and disappear, to walk through walls and mountains, to dive in and out of the earth, to walk on water, to fly in the lotus posture (which might explain the levitation attempts of TM students), to touch the sun and moon with one's hands, to physically visit the realm of the gods – the power to hear at a distance, the power to know others' minds, the power to remember past lives, and the power to see how beings fare according to their deeds. The eight attainments are the achievement and understanding of both physical form and formlessness, i.e. the spirit.
7. He must be an individual willing to sacrifice his life.
8. He must have great zeal.

Opposite: *The gates leading into a Buddhist temple, Nepal.* Below: *The Buddha sits with his disciples, all of whom became Arahants.*

This extraordinary person, having made his vow to achieve Buddha-nature for the sake of others, and whose destiny has been confirmed by the word of a living Buddha, sets out on his path for a journey that may last thousands of lifetimes, during which he continually perfects himself by cultivating the virtues of a Bodhisattva. The virtues are: ethics, renunciation, wisdom, effort, patience, truthfulness, resolution, love, and equanimity. Thus the main difference between an Arahant and a Bodhisattva is that the former discovers Nirvana in the presence of a Buddha, or through the study of Dharma as taught by the Buddha, whereas the Bodhisattva embarks on the long path out of compassion for others and their suffering, postponing his own attainment of Nirvana for many lifetimes.

The path of the Bodhisattva is open to both monks and lay people. The most famous lay Bodhisattva was Vimalkirty, to whom many Arahants came for instruction.

Below: *Two Arahants are portrayed with haloes symbolizing their enlightenment.*

Opposite: *Prayer stones placed by the side of a road, forming a natural temple.*

The Bodhisattva is a humanitarian saint. He brings light to those who are in darkness, dispels fear and brings encouragement, cures grief and gives joy, provides food for the hungry, clothes for the poor, a home for the homeless. In this sense, he shares a symbiotic relationship with those he helps: they aid him in his development of the virtues, and they are helped by him – in the short term by receiving what is needed, and in the long term by benefiting from the presence of a saint.

As the Bodhisattva ascends in his journey towards enlightenment he acquires powers which are, at least in our terms, miraculous. These include seeing and being blessed by a hundred Buddhas; living for a hundred eons; entering into and rising from a hundred meditative states; illuminating a hundred worlds.

As the Bodhisattva ascends higher these faculties are multiplied, so that in the next level he illuminates a thousand worlds, on the third level a hundred thousand, and so on. As he ascends his wisdom deepens, his virtues become purer. Because of his compassion the Bodhisattva does not fear the cycle of the Wheel of Karma and thus, once he has reached enlightenment, he does not dwell in that state but chooses to reincarnate, dedicating himself for eternity to the bettering of all beings.

THE DALAI LAMA
– A LIVING BUDDHIST SAINT

His Holiness, the Fourteenth Dalai Lama of Tibet, Tenzin Gyatso, is the spiritual and temporal ruler of the Tibetan people. He is also the reincarnation of one of the many Tibetan deities, Chenrezi, the Buddha of Compassion. He was born in 1935 into a peasant family in the village of Tankster, in the Tibetan province of Amdo, and his parents named him Lhamo Dhondrup. When he was two years old, a large group of important men arrived at Kumbum Monastery, which was a day's ride from his home. They were one of three search parties sent to find the latest incarnation of the Dalai Lama, for the previous one had died four years before in Lhasa. Rumors led the men to the small child in the village of Tankster and to their amazement, when they met him, he recognized one of the men in the secret party as being a lama of the Sera Monastery in Lhasa. The child also displayed all the bodily marks of the reincarnation of the god Cherenzi. Thus Lhamo Dhondrup came to be recognized as the Fourteenth Dalai Lama of Tibet and was taken to Lhasa where he underwent an intensive course of religious education.

In 1950, however, the world of the Tibetans began to crumble as Chinese armies invaded Tibet's eastern frontier. The Dalai Lama fled over the Himalayas to a village near the Indian border with Tibet, Dharamsala, which today is his exile headquarters.

The Dalai Lama is venerated by the Tibetan people and is acclaimed by the rest of the world as one of the most important religious figures today. In 1989 he was awarded the Nobel Peace Prize in recognition of his struggle for the liberation of Tibet. He has consistently opposed the use of violence, instead advocating peaceful solutions based upon tolerance and mutual respect in order to preserve the historical and cultural heritage of his people. This philosophy is based upon a great reverence for all living things and upon the concept of universal responsibility embracing all mankind as well as nature.

Opposite: *His Holiness, the Fourteenth Dalai Lama of Tibet, is a very powerful source of inspiration for our modern times.* Below: *The Dalai Lama leads the meditation in a Buddhist monastery in Italy.*

Saint Beuno's Church at Pistyll, Lleyn Peninsula, North Wales. According to tradition, the Saint's bones rest beneath the altar.

PART TWO

SAINTLY INTERVENTION

The Virgin and Child and eleven angels standing in a heavenly bed of
flowers. Wilton Diptych, National Gallery, London.

PART TWO
SAINTLY INTERVENTION

CHAPTER ONE

IS THERE HOPE?
A WHO'S WHO OF SAINTS AND GRACES GRANTED

Illuminated manuscript illustration of Saint Mary Magdalen, Bodleian Library, Oxford.

he success that saints have enjoyed throughout the centuries is primarily due to their role as intercessors between God and the human realm. Saints are traditionally believed to perform miracles, most often in the form of healings, and their relics hold the most wonder-working powers. The source of the cures, of course, is God, who uses the saint as His channel. In a symmetry of roles, saints would not exist without the faithful asking God for grace through their intercession. But miracles are few and far between, and it is popularly believed that it is the saint who chooses when and to whom the miracle should be granted.

The granting of graces, however, seems to be directly influenced by the depth of devotion and the number of prayers the devotee offers the chosen saint. The South of Italy and Spain, for example, have long been fruitful regions for the granting of wonders. This may be due to the essentially friendly nature of the relationship adopted by supplicants to their chosen saints, who are more like members of the family than superior beings. Images of saints are kept in special places, such as the kitchen, or on the bedside table. The devotee "visits" the saint in church, in order to converse about the events of the week: a fight with a lover, the sickness of a child, a death in the family, or whatever else is burdening the heart at that moment. These silent dialogues, taking the form of genuinely friendly conversations, end with a prayer. In times of great distress, the saint will

be asked to intercede using divine power in a situation which the petitioner feels cannot be resolved without such very special help.

Over the centuries, the communities of the faithful have, through trial and error, formulated a dictionary of those saints who have consistently granted their graces in different areas of need. Each saint catalogued here has a specialty: Saint Apollonia reputedly cures toothache more effectively than an aspirin, and Saint Helen disperses depression. The important thing, as always, is the sincerity of the petitioner's faith, for a saint will not be roused to action unless the prayer is heartfelt.

Opposite: *Saint Peter visits Saint Agatha.*

SAINT AGATHA, PATRON OF BREAST ILLNESSES

Saint Agatha was born of a noble family in Catania, Italy. She was reputedly very beautiful and devoted to the worship of God. Quintilian, a consul of Sicily, made her a proposal of engagement which she refused. She was thereafter arrested, her breasts cut off, and died as a martyr in the violent persecution against the Christians initiated by the Roman Emperor Decius in the year 250. Saint Agatha's intercession can be requested whenever a woman is suffering from an illness which affects the breasts, or, if she is facing an operation, she may petition for successful results.

THE RITUAL

The petitioner must offer three pink flowers and light a white candle every day, for nine days. During this period, it is advisable to avoid all confrontations with other women in the household. The prayer eliciting the saint's intercession will be made every morning:

"Saint Agatha, virgin and martyr,
you who knew suffering through your beauty and maintained faith in Christ,
please intercede for this humble servant who is afflicted by [the illness]
and who hopes to survive through your help
so that she will continue to venerate your name and glory.
Soothe my suffering and bring health to my body.
Amen."

THE OFFERING

Once the illness has been cured, or the operation is declared successful, the petitioner will thank Saint Agatha by "turning" her prayers on a rosary every day, for thirty days. The petitioner will also write her full name, draw a cross, and write the name of the saint and the word "thank you" on a pink ribbon, which will be buried in the garden next to a patch of blooming forget-me-nots. If it is the wrong season, then the petitioner will keep the ribbon until the flowers appear. The deeper the color of the forget-me-nots, the more sincere the offering will appear to the saint, as the color symbolizes the depth of suffering during illness.

Opposite: *Saint Anne and the Virgin Mary as a young girl.*

SAINT ANNE, PATRON OF PREGNANT WOMEN

Anne was the mother of the Virgin Mary. As exemplar of a pious mother, the intercession of Saint Anne can be requested by women to grant success and happiness in pregnancy.

THE RITUAL

Every morning upon waking, for the duration of the pregnancy, the petitioner will dip her finger in olive oil and draw three circles around her stomach. She will also prepare a small sachet containing a white ribbon with her name written on it, the petals from one carnation, some lavender, a pinch of sugar, a pearl, a lock of recently cut hair, and an ear of wheat. The sachet must then be put under the mattress, approximately at the position where the stomach rests during sleep. The petitioner will say the following words in the prayer while circling the stomach:

"Three divinities form the Holy Trinity, and make one God.
These three circles protect the life and development of a new being who will come
into the world in the will of the Father, the Son, and the Holy Ghost.
Please grant that all the beauty, intelligence, strength, and wisdom
center upon this new being, and that blessed Saint Anne help me during labor.
Please grant that this fruit of love will be protected in the same way as you helped
your daughter the Virgin Mary, and that with your protection and my humble
desire this being will become an example of virtue.
Holy Trinity, be abundant in your divine benediction of this humble servant
and ensure that the life engendered within me
starts with your blessing."

THE OFFERING

Once the baby is born, the petitioner will light a small candle every day, for forty days. The sachet will have to be thrown into the sea or a river. To protect the baby, the mother will lace the cot with a ribbon, onto which the name of the baby, a cross, and the words "Saint Anne" will be written.

Opposite: *Saint Anthony, by the Spanish painter Zurbarán, in the Palazzo Pitti, Florence.*

SAINT ANTHONY, PROTECTOR OF ANIMALS

Saint Anthony was born in Memphis, Egypt, around the year 251. He left his wealthy family and established his hermitage in the desert. There he reputedly died on Mount Kolzim, near the Red Sea, surrounded by other disciples and animals, in the year 356. The tradition of Saint Anthony's protection and love of animals has been maintained to this day, and it is said that no household caring for an animal will ever lack food if the Saint's protection is invoked.

THE RITUAL

Whenever an animal is ill, the petitioner can request good health by placing seven bowls of water next to seven candles. A laurel leaf, a pinch of salt, and a few drops of blessed oil will be thrown into each bowl. Lighting the candles, one must say the following prayer:

"Glorious Saint Anthony, who out of your goodness
made all animals into your brothers, and are thus honored as their patron,
please turn your eyes and blessing to this small animal who suffers from illness.
You know the loneliness of the desert, and you also know
the sadness in my heart which is caused by my impotence
in facing the illness which afflicts my companion.
Please free it from pain, and bring back its health
so that you too can enjoy its company in my household.
Your will be done."

The petitioner must then say two "Our Fathers" and one "Credo."

THE OFFERING

On the first day of the week during which this ritual is performed, the petitioner will throw the water of the first bowl into a larger bowl and at the same time he or she will say: "Monday, let my animal be cured." The same action and words are repeated throughout the rest of the week. Also, some of this water may be drunk by the animal, or the petitioner might pour some of it on its head or body.

Opposite: *Saint Apollonia holds a tooth extractor, in a fresco by Bernardino Luini (1475- c.1532) on the walls of her sanctuary in Saronno, Italy.*

Saint Apollonia, Healer of Toothaches

Saint Apollonia, a virgin, suffered and died as a martyr in Alexandria, Egypt, in an anti-Christian riot by the Alexandrian mob. Her assailants tortured her by extracting all her teeth with brute force, and she was put to death at the stake where she was burned alive. The nature of her martyrdom has made her a healer of toothache.

The Ritual

When suffering from acute toothache, the petitioner must prepare a mixture with white honey, a teaspoonful of cognac, and chopped parsley. A tablespoonful of the mixture is then applied to the painful area and the following prayer must be said:

"As the sea calms its fury, help me with my pain,
I ask you blessed Saint Apollonia.
Extinguish this fire that I now feel,
with the strength that sustained you in your suffering.
Please diminish my pain,
so that I may glorify your name in Heaven."

The Offering

When the toothache has been cured, the petitioner will thank the saint by mixing in a terracotta bowl a pinch of sea-salt, some petals from a white flower, powdered myrrh, chamomile, oil mixed with a few drops of lemon juice, and chopped cloves. The mixture will then be placed within a yellow sachet that can be applied to where the pain was felt. A small offering of twenty-one yellow flowers placed around a yellow candle must also be made to show gratitude to Saint Apollonia.

The Blessed Souls of Purgatory –
To Ensure Waking Up at a Particular Hour

If the petitioner needs to wake up at a certain hour and cannot rely upon a clock, then seven "Our Fathers" and seven "Hail Marys" must be said, asking that the souls of purgatory wake the petitioner at the requested hour. Rest can then be peaceful for the souls will grant this wish for sure. Upon waking, thanks must be given with seven "Our Fathers" and seven "Hail Marys." Every time this method is implemented seven suffering souls in purgatory will be liberated.

Opposite: *Souls being led into purgatory.*

SAINT AUGUSTINE, PATRON OF BONE WEAKNESS

The Spanish Saint Augustine was born paralyzed and, unable to walk, crawled on his knees. He surrendered to his handicap and showed goodness to all those around him. People felt great compassion for him and freely gave alms with which he eventually built a church in honor of Saint Martin. He was granted a miracle – his ailments disappeared and he was able to walk and live normally. He took the vows of priesthood out of gratitude.

THE RITUAL

The petitioner suffering from a bone ailment will prepare the following mixture: two ounces of oil, two ounces of rose essence, a few lemon flowers, a pinch of powdered cinnamon, sandalwood, six ounces of pure alcohol, and a pinch each of dried rue and valerian. This will make an excellent oil which can be massaged on the weak part of the body while saying the following prayer:

"Glorious Saint Augustine,
Servant of God Our Lord,
please place your hand upon my illness,
and keep the devil away from me.
In the same way as the stone opened
and delivered water for the sons of Israel to drink,
please deliver me, through your intercession,
from this illness which torments me.
I offer my pain to all the angels in Heaven,
to the prophets, and to all the men and women
who have suffered martyrdom in the name of God.
Please allow my faith and hope to make me feel
your divine love and your spiritual aid.
Amen."

The petitioner will then say three "Our Fathers" and one "Credo."

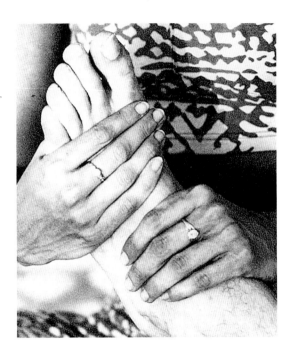

THE OFFERING

When the bones get stronger the offering to thank Saint Augustine will consist of burying a small wicker basket in the garden containing a black and a green ribbon tied with a piece of paper on which the name of the person is written. In the basket the petitioner will also put some oats, fingernails recently cut, an olive branch, oregano, and three old nails. The basket will have to be buried in a shady spot, away from wind currents. It is also good to bury a piece of paper bearing the name of the saint.

The martyrdom of Saint Barbara, by Lorenzo Lotto (1480-1556), in the Cappella Suardi, Trescore Balneario, Italy.

SAINT BARBARA, PATRON OF STORMS

According to legend, Saint Barbara was murdered by her own father when she would not abandon the Christian faith. She died a virgin and martyr. Saint Barbara is the patron of artillery and her help can be called upon when stormy weather savages the land.

THE RITUAL

When a storm starts raging all the members of the household must come together in one room and, after closing all the doors and windows, a white candle must be lit and placed in the middle of a round table. One person must then say the following prayer aloud:

"Blessed Saint Barbara,
your name is written in Heaven
with paper and holy water,
and on the cross of our death.
Send away the storm
and bring peace to our household. Amen."

THE OFFERING

Once the prayer has been said three times and the storm is starting to pass, the candle must be extinguished and wrapped in a white cloth. The petitioners shall also draw crosses on the doors and windows of the house, and place an olive branch in the kitchen window to honor the saint.

The martyrdom of Saint Bartholomew, by Stephan Lochner, in the Pinacoteca della Città Vaticana.

SAINT BARTHOLOMEW, PATRON OF WOMEN IN LABOR

According to legend Saint Bartholomew was one of the twelve apostles chosen by Jesus to disseminate his teaching worldwide, and he reputedly lived on the shores of the Black Sea. He was persecuted for being a Christian and died as a martyr when orders were given to have his head cut off.

THE RITUAL

In order to ask for the protection of Saint Bartholomew during labor, the petitioner will light two candles, one representing the child about to be born and the other the mother. The petitioner will also say the following prayer requesting Saint Bartholomew's intercession:

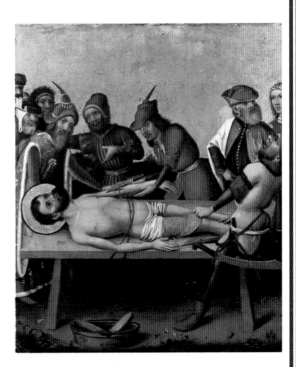

> *"Saint Bartholomew rose,*
> *washed his hands and feet,*
> *and said to Jesus,*
> *'Lord, I shall come with you.'*
> *'No,' replied Jesus,*
> *'I must give you a gift that no other man has.*
> *In every household where your name is mentioned*
> *no lightning shall fall,*
> *no mother shall die in labor,*
> *no child shall die of fright.'*
> *Amen."*

The petitioner will also say three "Our Fathers."

THE OFFERING

When the baby is born, the mother will light three candles surrounded by twenty-one white carnations for seven days. The candles will burn for one hour every day. At the end of the week, the candles and the flowers must be wrapped in a red cloth and buried at night in a pot with chamomile seeds. If the chamomile plant grows, it will mean that the baby will grow healthily and happily.

Opposite: *Horseman bearing the scales of justice. Detail from an eleventh-century Spanish manuscript.*

SAINT BASIL, PATRON OF CAUSES OF JUSTICE

Saint Basil was perhaps one of the most prolific authors of Church doctrine. He died in 379 when he was fifty years of age.

THE RITUAL

If the petitioner has been wrongly accused or is concerned about the result of a law trial, he or she can ask for the help of Saint Basil by lighting three red candles and burning incense with spices in a terracotta bowl. Adding sea salt and a few drops of holy water into the bowl, the petitioner must say the following prayer:

> *"Lord Jesus, I ask you to remedy my problem,*
> *and for Saint Basil to intercede;*
> *I place my faith and hope on the outcome of this trial I will endure.*
> *Please direct your presence and benediction to this household [or matter].*
> *In the same way as when you came into this world you blessed everything,*
> *and blessed the house of Zachary when visiting him,*
> *please accept the petition of this servant and bless me.*
> *Amen."*

The petitioner must say the prayer of "Our Father" once.

THE OFFERING

When the trial meets with success, the petitioner must thank Saint Basil by putting in a small red sachet a piece of paper inscribed with the name of the saint, and three crosses drawn beneath, with the name of the petitioner written under the crosses. This small cloth bag will also contain three laurel leaves, and a pinch each of valerian and oregano. The petitioner will carry this bag for thirty days, at the end of which its contents will be burned and the resulting ashes buried.

Opposite: *Saint Cecilia, by Raffaello (1483-1520), in the Pinacoteca Nazionale, Bologna.*

SAINT CECILIA, PATRON OF MUSICIANS

There are no clear historical records of this saint, but by the year 545 she was honored as a martyr. Since the sixteenth century she has been regarded as the patron saint of musicians.

THE RITUAL

In order to request the protection of Saint Cecilia during a concert performance, or for a music examination, the petitioner must write the name of the saint on a white ribbon, and his or her own name on a yellow ribbon. The two ribbons are then tied to a green candle into which the petitioner must stick two laurel leaves. When the candle is lit, one must say the following prayer:

"Oh glorious Saint Cecilia!
You died loving your martyrdom,
and accepted the sacrifice in order to protect your virginity.
I ask you to help me in this test I am going to undertake,
upon which my honor and work rely.
Listen to my prayers, Saint Cecilia,
and I will play music in your name.
Let me venerate you always in the glory of
the Father, the Son, and the Holy Ghost.
Amen."

THE OFFERING

When the musician meets success in his or her task, the ribbons and the candle must be buried in a big plant pot filled with pink flowers, or in a garden. The laurel leaves will be burned and the ashes kept in a small wooden box. If the aid of Saint Cecilia is requested several times, it is advisable to collect all the ashes from the burning of the leaves in this same box.

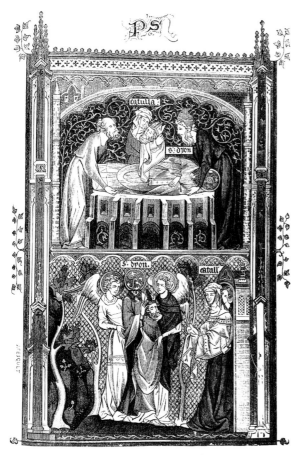

SAINT DENNIS, HEALER OF HEADACHES

Saint Paul converted Dennis to the Christian faith and made him bishop of the church in Athens. Dennis, however, was persecuted and ordered to be put to death. Legend tells that his faith was so strong that he suffered several martyrdoms: he was tied to a stake and a fire was lit, but he would not burn. He was put on a cross and beaten, and he would not die. Thus, in the last attempt to kill him, his head was cut off, but it is said that he picked up his own head and walked for several miles guided by an angel to the place where he wished to die.

In case of a severe headache, the petitioner can dip a white ribbon into rainwater, and place in its center a few carnation petals, some crushed garlic, and a pinch of powdered cinnamon. The ribbon can then be tied around the head and the following prayer said:

"Blessed Saint Dennis,
please intercede on my behalf with the Supreme
and cure this headache
which is burdening my spirit,
so that I may also be,
like you were in your martyrdom,
clear in my thoughts
and be able to venerate our Lord.
Amen."

THE OFFERING

When the headache has been cured, the ribbon with the garlic and cinnamon must be kept for three days. The ribbon then can be thrown away, but the garlic must be preserved in pure water and wrapped in a green sachet or cloth. This will be a strong amulet to prevent further headaches.

Medieval woodcut of Saints Cosmas and Demian.

COSMAS·DAMIANVS

SAINT DEMIAN, PATRON OF LOST OBJECTS

Demian was archbishop in Besançon, France, between 624 and 660. He died martyred in North Africa where he had led an expedition with his disciples. His name means "to give," and if his intercession is requested Saint Demian will return lost objects.

THE RITUAL

The petitioner must tie the four corners of a white handkerchief and throw it up in the air in the room where he or she believes the object was last seen. When tying the knots, the petitioner must say the following prayer:

"Saint Demian,
I tie your eggs,
and if [say the name of the lost object] does not appear,
I will not untie them again.
Please come to my aid."

Then say one "Credo."

THE OFFERING

Once the object has been found, untie each knot of the handkerchief while saying a "Credo" for each one. Then light four white candles positioned in a square shape.

SAINT HELEN, HEALER OF DEPRESSIONS

Helen was born in the county of York, England. She married a Roman emperor and had churches built over the Holy Sepulcher in Jerusalem, and over the cave where Jesus was born in Bethlehem. She also retrieved the cross on which Jesus died.

If one suffers from depression, then the aid of Saint Helen can be requested by carrying a small green sachet containing a piece of paper with the name of the saint written on it, three loose nails previously nailed into wood, part of an evergreen plant, a lock of hair, and a medallion or a paper image of the Saint. The sachet must be carried always, and the following prayer requesting Saint Helen's help must be said every night:

"Glorious Saint Helen, our protector,
please intercede from Heaven on my behalf,
I venerate your name and ask you
to grant me the grace to imitate you,
the strength in my soul and feelings to invoke you,
so that I may thank you for bringing aid to me."

To thank the saint the petitioner will say seven "Credos" for seven nights and offer a small cross to her statue if there exists a church in her honor in the neighborhood.

Above: *Saint Helen, by Paolo Veronese.*

SAINT EXPEDITE, BRINGER OF MONEY

In order never to lack money, the petitioners must keep a print portraying the saint with some coins at the bottom of a drawer, or wherever money is normally kept. One must make sure that there is always at least one coin offered to Saint Expedite in gratitude. When money is needed the following prayer will help:

"I ask you, Saint Expedite, to aid me in my financial difficulties. Let your strength and support protect my income and help me to obtain enough money so that I will not suffer need and want. Please let peace and enjoyment reign in my household. I ask you and pray that my wishes be granted, and glorify your intercession.
Amen."

THE OFFERING

In order to thank the saint the petitioner will give alms to a child, an elderly person, or to a pregnant woman. Every day the following prayer can be said so that the petitioner will never be in need:

"I trust you, Saint Expedite
to place your good hand upon everything I need."

Above: *Two Tax-gatherers, by Marinus van Reymerswaele.*

Opposite: *Allegory of Love – "Unfaithfulness," by Paolo Veronese.*

SAINT ELISABETH, PATRON OF WIVES WITH UNFAITHFUL HUSBANDS

Elisabeth was born in 1271 and when she was twelve she married Dennis, King of Portugal. During her marriage Elisabeth suffered greatly because of the infidelities of her husband and treated his many bastard children so well that people called her "Angel of Peace." When the King died, she became a nun of the Franciscan order, and died in 1336. Pope Urban VIII canonized her in 1626.

If a woman is suffering greatly as a result of her husband's infidelity, she can request the aid of Saint Elisabeth by tying a pink ribbon, approximately a meter long, around the ring finger of her left hand. The ribbon will bear the name of the petitioner and the name of her husband, written one after the other continuously. One must dip the finger in bleach, untie the ribbon and bury it in a pot with white flowers. The following prayer requests Saint Elisabeth's intercession in the matter:

"Oh Saint Elisabeth, your love of God sustained you
in your hurt with your husband and kept you loyal and sweet in your hope.
I ask you strength of heart and that my husband be tender and faithful,
that he not leave my path, but walk with me at his side with a firm hand,
without falling into the Devil's temptation.
Give me strength and attend to my need."

This prayer must be said every Friday at night, for nine consecutive weeks.

THE OFFERING

To thank Saint Elisabeth for the aid received, the petitioner must during seven consecutive spring evenings, by the light of the moon, place the petals of seven carnations into a glass of water. The petitioner shall start the offering on the waxing phase of the moon, and after the seven days have passed, she will place the petals into a hand-sewn sachet and let them dry. When this is done, the sachet must be placed in the husband's drawer, amid his underwear, and the petitioner will sprinkle eau de cologne in each corner of the drawer. If for any reason the sachet must be thrown away, then it must be burned and the ashes thrown into flowing water.

The petitioner must also thank Saint Elisabeth every night before going to sleep with the following words: "Thank you, Saint Elisabeth, for your help and faith, make my husband stay with me always."

Opposite: *Saint George slaying the dragon, by Gustave Moreau.*

SAINT GEORGE – TO BLESS A NEW HOME

Saint George was reputedly born in Cappadocia and was a soldier in the Roman army. Legend tells that he killed a dragon in order to save a beautiful virgin. He was martyred at Lydda during the persecutions of Diocletian, and is today the patron saint of England.

THE RITUAL

In order to bless a new home, the petitioner must enter every room, before any furniture has been moved into it, carrying a loaf of bread under one arm, a piece of coal, a pinch of sea salt and a fresh sprig of parsley in one hand, and the image of Saint George in the other. The following prayer will elicit the blessing of the saint:

> *"In the name of the Lord and Jesus,*
> *with the strength of the Holy Ghost and of Saint George,*
> *whom I promise to worship eternally,*
> *I ask for the blessing of this home.*
> *Keep away bad spirits,*
> *and make sure that in every corner of this house*
> *we will find hope for eternal glory.*
> *Please let us not be without bread to nourish us,*
> *coal to keep us warm, salt to purify us,*
> *and the magic of herbs to help us.*
> *In the name of Saint George who fought the dragon,*
> *let the evil forces be conquered*
> *and the good spirits win."*

THE OFFERING

Once the prayer has been said all the ingredients mentioned above must be put into a bag, adding rice, sugar, coffee, a laurel leaf, three copper coins, and an ear of wheat. The bag must be kept in the pantry or in the kitchen cupboard where food is stored.

SAINT JOAN OF ARC – TO OVERCOME FEAR

Saint Joan of Arc is the protector of women in distress, and her help can be called for in moments of fear.

THE RITUAL

Write on a blue ribbon the name of the saint and the words "Help Me!" Roll up the ribbon and place it in a sachet with chamomile, an unpeeled clove of garlic, powdered sandalwood, and the dried petals of a red rose. This sachet must be kept with personal objects, or inside the woman's bag. Every time the petitioner is afraid either because someone is following her, or she is threatened, or facing a tense situation, she will cross the fingers of both hands and say:

> *"Courageous Saint Joan*
> *come to my aid*
> *I feel impotent*
> *protect me now!*
> *Send the danger away,*
> *lady, give me strength,*
> *I feel you present as my protector."*

THE OFFERING

Having received proof of the protection of the saint in a moment of fear, the petitioner will wear a ring made from copper on the little finger of the left hand during nine full days. Each day she will light a candle dedicated to Saint Joan of Arc. After the nine days she will bury the ring in a pot planted with a green plant without flowers.

Saint Joan of Arc.

SAINT LUKE, PATRON OF BACHELORS

Luke was born in Antioch and was the only gentile apostle. He was a doctor, and preached the apostolic works alongside Saint Paul. In his work, both written and preached, he specifically addressed women and the poor. When Saint Paul was arrested, Luke went with him to Rome and remained his companion until his martyrdom. Luke died a natural death at the age of eighty-four, and his relics were brought to Constantinople in the year 357 CE.

THE RITUAL

In order to foresee a beloved in a dream or to foretell whether destiny will grant love to the petitioner, on the eve of 18th October, the day Saint Luke is celebrated, the following prayer must be said.

> *"Blessed Saint Luke,*
> *I ask Jesus Christ if in my destiny*
> *it is written that I will meet a faithful companion.*
> *You shall be my go-between,*
> *and I, your devout servant.*
> *Amen."*

The petitioner will gather calendula flowers, a sprig of marjoram, and a pinch of paprika. The ingredients must be burned by fire, powdered, and boiled with honey and olive oil. From this mixture is made a cream which the petitioner will rub onto the hands, the feet, the back of the neck, and the forehead before sleep. He must also speak the words: "Saint Luke be kind to me and let me dream of my true and great love."

Saint Luke, from a medieval manuscript.

THE OFFERING

If from the intercession of the saint the petitioner ceases to be a bachelor, his dream having been granted in reality, then he must plant a small tree and draw his name and the name of his new beloved on the earth by the trunk. The ritual must be performed on a Tuesday which coincides with a night of waxing moon.

DON DE M. PERCY MOORE TURNER, 1948
EN SOUVENIR DE M. PAUL JAMOT

GEORGES DE LA TOUR 1593-1652
SAINT JOSEPH CHARPENTIER

Opposite: Saint Joseph and the young Jesus in his carpenter's workshop, by Georges de La Tour (1593-1652), in the Louvre, Paris.

SAINT JOSEPH, PATRON OF GOOD DEATHS

Joseph was chosen by God to be the earthly father of Jesus for his humble, peaceful and faithful nature, for being a hard worker, and because he would not consummate his marriage with Mary before Jesus was born. In 1870 Pope Pius IX made him a patron saint of the Church.

THE RITUAL

In order to be granted a peaceful death by Saint Joseph, the petitioner must say a prayer on the first day of every month, kneeling down, with arms outstretched as though crucified, facing the image of Saint Joseph and with a lit candle. The petitioner can also offer a red flower. The prayer is as follows:

"Oh beloved Saint Joseph!
For the love you had for Jesus and Mary,
for your pain and pleasure,
for your great merit,
please be compassionate towards me
in the terrible trance of death.
Please give my heart calmness and peace.
Please give my soul serenity,
faith in the goodness of God,
and resignation in surrendering my will to His.
Please grant me the sacraments at the hour of death,
the aid and grace that will liberate my soul
and open the doors of Paradise."

THE OFFERING

At the moment of death, those present may say this prayer and an image of Saint Joseph can be placed in the coffin before burial.

Opposite: *Saint Mary Magdalen, by Titian (1477-1576), in the Galleria Palatina, Florence.*

SAINT MARY MAGDALEN, PATRON OF LOST WOMEN

Mary Magdalen was popularly believed to be a sinner, who brought goodness and virtue into her own life after meeting Jesus. She also became a devoted disciple.

THE RITUAL

If a woman feels lost in her ways and wishes to return to a life of virtue, she can ask for Saint Mary Magdalen's help by sewing a small red sachet, which she will keep on her body for twenty-one consecutive days. When sewing it with red thread she must say the following words:

> *"I wish for good luck to be with me,*
> *and for my life to be channeled into a virtuous path."*

The petitioner will fill the sachet with a pink ribbon bearing the name of the saint, a small crucifix, powdered sandalwood, the rind of a lemon, aniseed, and the petals of a pink carnation. This prayer must be said in order to elicit the saint's protection:

> *"In the same way as you followed the steps of the Master,*
> *abandoned a life marked by sin,*
> *and embraced the light, please bring light to my own steps,*
> *so that I may be guided forward*
> *without falling into the temptations of the Devil and the flesh.*
> *Please grant me your protection*
> *so that I may have the strength to overcome*
> *all the difficulties and hard work this situation presents.*
> *Blessed Saint Mary Magdalen,*
> *please do not abandon me in my pain."*

THE OFFERING

When the problems have been resolved, the petitioner will burn the small sachet and bury the ashes in a pot with red flowers, which should be watered for twenty-one consecutive days.

Opposite: *Saint Thomas Aquinas, doctor of the Church and "universal teacher."*

SAINT THOMAS AQUINAS, PATRON OF STUDENTS

Saint Thomas Aquinas was perhaps the greatest scholar of evangelical doctrine. He died in a monastery in Fossanove, Italy, in 1274 and was canonized in 1323.

THE RITUAL

The student must fast for twenty-four hours the day before an important examination. On the eve of the examination, he or she must place seven red flowers and as many candles as the subjects to be tested in the exam before a print bearing the image of Saint Thomas. The candles must be left to burn out during the night, and the remains wrapped in a white cloth. This will be the talisman to bring good luck during the examination and the student will keep this wrapping in his or her pocket.

The next morning, before attending the exam, the petitioner will throw the talisman and the seven red flowers in flowing water and say the following prayer:

"Blessed Saint Thomas,
please listen to my plea.
I elicit your help to make sure
that my memory does not fail me,
and that my nerves stay calm,
so that I may be successful in my exam.
I trust in your influence, oh blessed Saint Thomas."

The petitioner will also say one "Our Father" and one "Hail Mary."

THE OFFERING

If the exam is successful, then the petitioner will thank Saint Thomas by giving alms to seven paupers, and by giving a poor child some clothes, toys, or food.

SAINT VALENTINE, PATRON OF LOVERS

Valentine was a priest in Rome who, during the reign of the emperor Claudius II, suffered martyrdom because he would not renounce the Christian faith. His head was cut off and, later, a church was built on the site where he died.

The name Valentine signifies valor and for many centuries lovers have appealed to the saint for courage and strength when facing adversity or difficulties in their love affairs.

THE RITUAL

If the petitioner is suffering because the course of love is inhibited by forces beyond his or her control, then he or she will say the following prayer to elicit the Saint's intercession:

"Blessed Saint Valentine, please accept my petition with the same compassion and interest that you showed in your love of God. I feel today the certainty of my love for [say the name of the beloved]. I thus ask you to support my petition so that unconditional love may blossom, and our union remain intact for centuries to come. Please allow the valor of your name to give us strength, and protect us against evil forces trying to separate us. Amen."

The petitioner will say three "Our Fathers."

THE OFFERING

Gather some small flowers in a forest and place them in the shape of a cross next to two green candles. Then place by them a photograph of yourself and your beloved or, if this is not possible, a piece of paper with the two names written on it in the shape of a cross. Allow the candles to burn out, and then put them, with the photographs and the flowers, inside a wooden box.

Above: *Lovers call for the help of Saint Valentine when facing difficulties in affairs of the heart.* Opposite: *The Holy Family. Beneath them are the prophets Isaiah, Jeremiah, Ezekiel and Daniel. Stained glass window in Cologne cathedral.*

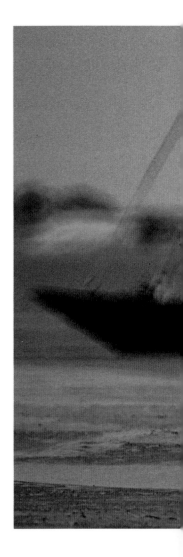

Catholic saints are in a unique position to intercede with God on behalf of mankind; devotion, in the form of prayers, offerings, and rituals, is thus almost always guaranteed to bring solace for everyday problems. In other religious traditions, however, we find that saints and holy beings not only do not have the same function as Catholic saints, but that there is no ritual tradition of drawing upon saintly help to relieve the pains of one's earthly existence. This is most notably so in Judaism where models of faith, wisdom, and piety are provided to inspire the faithful to cultivate those qualities within themselves for the common good. On religious festivities and holy days, such as the weekly Sabbath or annual Passover, prayers are directed to God to thank Him for his bounty and benevolence. The notion of asking a holy being for intercession in everyday affairs is anathema to Jews. The faithful may, instead, seek the advice of the elders and rabbis whose function is to care for the well-being of the whole community.

Similarly, in Islam, prayers and remembrance of Allah are recited daily; the faithful may call for God's blessing upon home, marriage, and family, to relieve their anxieties at work, to safeguard them during long journeys, and on other aspects of human life. Here again, the devout Muslim applies directly to God – even the Prophet Mohammad is unable to intercede on behalf of the individual, and the idea that he should do so is thoroughly unholy.

A devout Muslim prays on the bank of the Nile.

India's saints, on the other hand, are the wandering sadhus and sannyasins who live at the periphery of Hindu society, and yet are supported by it – to fill a saint's begging bowl is an act of virtue for all Hindus. Anyone can walk up to them, seek advice, learn something, and then return, hopefully wiser, to the secular world. Spiritual gurus, the pinnacle of wisdom within the Hindu religious framework, often have a very personal and intimate contact with their devotees. The teaching is passed from the guru to the disciple at the "satsang," the meeting with the master. During the satsang the master may lecture on a particular topic or give an interpretation of sacred scriptures; what is most important, however, is not the words he speaks to the gathering of his disciples but his physical presence. It is this presence that enables the disciple to enter a state of meditation which would be more difficult to achieve on his or her own.

Getting acquainted with the state of profound stillness known as meditation is a very important part of the transmission of wisdom. Once the disciple knows meditation, he or she can recall it just by thinking of the master. Eventually, when meditation is fully known, there is no longer any need for the master either to be present or to be remembered from a distance.

Hindu sages, moreover, may transmit insight in darsan (literally meaning "seeing") by touching the body of the disciple. This touching, or "shaktipat" sends a rush of energy through the the disciple's body.

Buddhist monks in meditation, Thailand.

The shock of this energy transmission breaks all conditioned thought in the mind and gives fresh and enlightened sight, even if only momentarily. The disciples show the master their readiness to receive his full teaching in the act of "namaste:" this is the traditional Indian greeting, performed by placing both palms together and bowing deeply to the saint. Touching the saint's feet is also an outward sign of deep devotion and gratefulness for the blessings received.

Buddhist worship is deeply ritualistic; mantras, salutations to the Buddhas, and chants are the most common forms of devotional worship (called "puja"). The Sevenfold Puja, for instance, is a series of verses, each expressing a different emotional mood, which will bring blessing upon whoever chants it. Usually puja is performed in a room specially set aside for meditation, or in a temple; the room may be adorned with fresh flowers and lit by candles. The worshippers may sit cross-legged on the floor and direct their prayers to a Tibetan "thangka," a painting of the Buddha.

1. Worship

With mandarava, blue lotus, and jasmine,
With all flowers pleasing and fragrant,
And with garlands skillfully woven,
I pay honor to the princes of the Sages,
so worthy of veneration.
I envelop them in clouds of incense,
Sweet and penetrating;
I make them offerings of food, hard and soft,
And pleasing kinds of liquids to drink.
I offer them lamps encrusted with jewels,
Festooned with golden lotus.
On the paving, sprinkled with perfume,
I scatter handfuls of beautiful flowers.

In this first verse, the worshipper expresses gratitude for the existence of higher values as represented by the Buddha.

2. Salutation

As many atoms as there are
In the thousand million worlds,
So many times I make reverent salutation
To all the Buddhas of the Three Eras,
To the Saddharma,
And to the excellent Community.
I pay homage to the shrines,
and places in which Bodhisattvas have been.
I make profound obeyance to the Teachers,
And those to whom respectful salutation is due.

With this verse, the worshipper expresses gratitude for the gifts brought to him by the wisdom of the Buddha, the Dharma (sacred scriptures) and the community. The worshipper should bow while reciting his salutations.

3. Going for Refuge

This very day
I go for my refuge
To the powerful protectors,
Whose purpose is to guard the universe;
The mighty conquerors who overcome
*   suffering everywhere.*
Wholeheartedly also I take my refuge
In the Dharma they have ascertained,
Which is the abode of security against the
*   rounds of rebirth.*
Likewise in the host of Bodhisattvas
I take my refuge.

This verse expresses commitment – the worshipper's commitment to becoming the Buddha, following the Dharma, and living in harmony with the community of fellow seekers.

4. Confession of Faults

The evil which I have heaped up
Through my ignorance and foolishness –
Evil in the world of everyday experience,
As well as evil in understanding and intelligence –
All that I acknowledge to the Protectors.
Standing before them
With hands raised in reverence,
And terrified of suffering,
I pay salutations again and again.
May the Leaders receive this kindly,
Just as it is, with its many faults!
What is not good, O Protectors,
I shall not do again.

This verse acknowledges the mistakes made by the conditioned mind. The worshipper asks for forgiveness and resolves not to act out of foolishness and ignorance.

5. Rejoicing in Merit

I rejoice with delight
In the good done by all beings,
Through which they obtain rest
With the end of suffering.
May those who have suffered be happy!
I rejoice in the release of beings
From the sufferings of the rounds of existence;
I rejoice in the nature of the Bodhisattva
And the Buddha,
Who are Protectors.
I rejoice in the arising of the Will to Enlightenment,
And the Teaching:
Those Oceans which bring happiness to all beings,
And are the abode of welfare of all beings.

The worshipper here rejoices in the good done by all beings everywhere. In this stage of the puja one accumulates positive energy.

6. Entreaty and Supplication

Saluting them with folded hands
I entreat the Buddhas in all the quarters:
May they make shine the lamp of the Dharma
For those wandering in the suffering of delusion!
With hands folded in reverence
I implore the conquerors desiring to enter Nirvana:
May they make shine the lamp here for endless ages,
so that life in this world does not grow dark.

In this verse the worshipper admits his or her need for guidance; the Buddhas are asked to teach the Dharma and to light the way for all seekers.

Above: *In the act of offering puja the self is purified.*

7. Transference of Merit and Self-Surrender

May the merit gained in my acting thus
Go to the alleviation of the suffering of all beings.
My personality throughout my existences,
My possessions, and my merit in all three ways,
I give up without regard for myself
For the benefit of all beings.
Just as the earth and other elements
Are serviceable in many ways
To the infinite number of beings
Inhabiting limitless space; so may I become
That which maintains all beings
Situated throughout space,
so long as all have not attained
To peace.

This is the most beautiful verse in the whole puja; here the worshipper transfers the merit accumulated through performing the puja to all beings of the universe; this verse gives the worshipper a glimpse into the selfless nature of all Bodhisattvas.

Drawn from:
The Puja Book, A Book of Devotional Texts,
Windhorse Publications, Glasgow, 1990.

Above: *Offerings at the feet of the Buddha.*

Below: *Mount Brandon, County Kerry, Ireland, a popular site of pilgrimage.*

Opposite: *A Chinese devotee carries flowers in a procession.*

CHAPTER TWO

MIRACLES AND PILGRIMAGES

We have seen that the notion of sainthood proves problematic when applied across the various world religions, for each individual tradition expresses this notion very differently. Christianity, with its strictly established institutions and rules, has a concept of saintliness which is sharply delineated. Judaism, with its lack of spiritual and institutional hierarchy, has no official notion of sainthood whatsoever, nor does Islam. Hinduism and Buddhism center upon the concept of the perfectibility of mankind, and thus have established systems within which the individual may come to his or her full flowering, embracing a higher nature to which even the gods are subordinated.

Despite this diversity of views, sainthood has survived within each tradition – sometimes on the periphery, sometimes without official recognition. Exceptional individuals have tickled the religious interest of their contemporaries at different times and in different ways. If it is difficult to find common themes in their various messages when they are examined cross-culturally, then perhaps we should direct our attention to the popular recognition of sainthood – to the many cults that have arisen as axes of spiritual reference, drawing thousands of devotees to experience first-hand the divine essence.

The most popular attributes of the saints are the wonders and miracles that prove the "otherness" of their nature, as though God were acting from within

Below: *The age-old Croagh Patrick pilgrimage to Saint Patrick's retreat on Cruachan Aigli in County Mayo, Ireland.* Opposite: *Hindu pilgrims in a procession.*

these chosen individuals to bring about the greater well-being of the community. Miracles and wonders cannot be explained. They are part of a divine plan which humanity is not privy to, and as such they leave us in awe and deepen our willingness to believe and follow the religious paradigm. If anything at all has made saints famous it is their performance of miracles. Devotees are willing to travel great distances in order to feel and see for themselves the workings of the divine. The greater the power to perform miracles, the more popular the shrine and the saint. Thus, the tradition of pilgrimage – a spiritual journey during which the faithful might cleanse the spirit, renew the

faith, and ask for divine intercession – is as ancient as sainthood itself. Both pilgrimages and miracles are very important features of all the major religious traditions – Christian, Jewish, Islamic, Hindu, and Buddhist. Truly speaking, for the Eastern religions of Hinduism and Buddhism miracles are but an outward sign of the progress of an individual toward higher inner virtues. In Christianity, by contrast, miracles are a proof of saintliness. But the common ground shared by miracles across all the traditions is that they are an extraordinary manifestation of power. And such power belongs only to certain individuals who light the flame of the divine and keep it burning amongst ordinary human folk.

A religious procession made in spring to bring fertility to the fields, on the
Adriatic island of Susak.

MIRACLES AND WONDERS

Not unnaturally, because miracle-working is an
essential ingredient in defining a Christian saint,
these events have been most widely recorded in the
hagiographical collections and canonization
inquiries written over the centuries within this
religious tradition.

Broadly speaking, miracles and wonders fall
within three categories: healings, nature miracles,
and prophecies or visions. Of these, by far the most
popular are the healing miracles, somehow
symptomatic of humanity's need to be purged from
ills and evils and to be filled with the same spirit and
light as the saints themselves possess.

Many of the healings recorded in association with
Christian saints occur after the venerable person's
death. The miraculous healings are, in this particular
context, proof that he or she is in heaven and is
interceding there on behalf of supplicants on earth.

Healing miracles became increasingly popular
during the Middle Ages, between approximately 500
and 1500 CE, and the process of certifying them grew
more and more elaborate. One of the earliest
compilations of miraculous accounts was Gregory of
Tours' collection in the sixth century, and the
popularity of such accounts grew right up to the
Golden Legend collection assembled by Jacob of
Voragine during the thirteenth century. These stories
strengthened the belief of the faithful that the saints
cared for each individual, and that no one was alone in
the face of the terrible diseases and plagues of the time.

Miraculous cures by the saints could be made manifest in a number of ways: Saint Molua, for instance, breathed onto a dumb girl and enabled her to talk; a saintly kiss or the application of saintly saliva was believed to cure leprosy. The modesty of Saint Gerald of Aurillac prevented him from performing miracles directly, but the sick who lived within the range of his travels would steal the water he had washed in and use it to cure ills. A lame child, it was reported, arranged with friends to acquire the water from Gerald's servants and sprinkled it on his useless legs, which immediately were able to carry the boy as any normal legs should.

Relics were also a powerful agent through which miraculous healings occurred, and the shrines in which they were preserved became holy sites of pilgrimage. The events reported in association with relics range from the sublimely dramatic to the astonishingly mundane. In the former category we learn of a woman who, suffering from severe head pains and deafness, traveled to the shrine of Saint Thomas Becket, at Canterbury, in England. There, as she stood in prayer, she experienced a very severe burst of pain and according to her report after the event, felt as though many twigs of wood were being snapped within her head into small pieces. While in this state she called out to God, and huge amounts of pus flooded from her ears as though the internal affliction was shedding its poison. This was followed by copious blood, after which her hearing returned and evidently the head pains ceased.

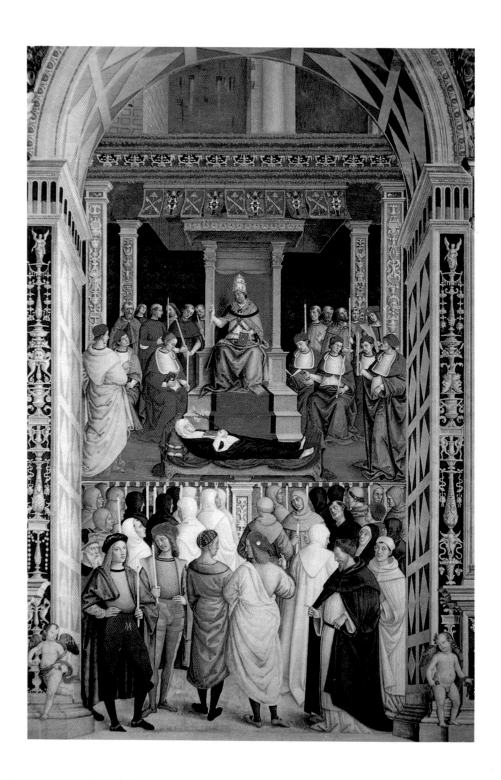

Saints were also known to have the ultimate healing power – the ability to bring the dead back to life. One curious instance of this is reported in the life of Saint Catherine of Siena. When she learned that a woman had died without receiving the sacraments, Saint Catherine remained by the side of the body, swearing that she would not move until the woman returned to life. The miracle transpired very quickly.

The extent of miraculous healings was not just restricted to curing illnesses, but also took on other forms, notably that of exorcising or banishing malignant souls. Much of the sickness present during the early medieval era in Europe was attributed to the presence of the devil or one of his numerous minions, and the power of the saints was often called upon in such cases. Martin of Tours, a French saint, was reported to have entered a house in which there were demons. He stood at the door and instructed the dark residents to depart, whereupon one of them took possession of the household cook who proceeded to bite and scratch others around him. Martin thrust his fingers into the cook's mouth and effectively "dared" him to bite them. The cook darted backwards, "as if he had taken a white-hot iron in his mouth." And because the demon could not escape from the cook's mouth, he was discharged from his bowels instead!

The nature miracles of the saints were manifested most often in their extraordinary power over the elements. Bizarre early medieval reports, written at the height of the popularity of the saints, told that saints could sink to the bottom of rivers or lakes and remain there without air for days; or they could cause the same lakes to dry up completely. Items in their possession would not be dampened by heavy

Opposite: *Saint Nicholas, who started to fast while still a baby at his mother's breast.* Right: *Saint Patrick, the patron saint of Ireland.*

falls of rain, and their ability to walk or kneel upon water was legendary. One such was seen to carry a heavy statue of the Virgin Mary across water and even leave a set of footprints behind!

Saints were furthermore reported to produce fire from fingertips, mouths, and noses, putting the heat to good effect in the case of Saint Comgall who breathed upon icicles in order to defrost a house. Some saints were even said to slow down the sun's passage through the heavens or hang their clothes upon sunbeams to make them dry.

Finally, the last category of saintly miracles is that of visions and prophecies. Saints were considered to be special friends of God, and in this privileged position they were believed to be an integral part of the divine plan devised for humanity. Thus, they could see and foretell events to which the rest of humanity were blind.

Admittedly, saintly prophecies dealt with both relevant and irrelevant matters. Saint Godric, for instance, always knew how many people would come to visit him each day, and several other saints were able to discern the thoughts of forthcoming sins in the minds of the unfortunates around them.

In some cases, certain holy individuals did not conform to our expectations of saintly behavior, as when Saint Patrick is said to have cursed the fish in an Irish lake because they would not submit to being caught (and presumably eaten by Saint Patrick). Saint Comgall caused thieves to be blinded as they attempted to steal from his home, keeping them in this state until they admitted their guilt.

The peculiarity of some saints has also been shown in their extraordinary and often precocious maturity. The concept of the *puer senex*, or aged child, is popular in hagiographical studies. Some cried from inside the womb, and stood immediately after birth, while others jumped enthusiastically into the baptismal font and dipped themselves in holy water. Babies learned to write within three days of birth, were born with monastic tonsures, or wobbled off to monasteries within moments of learning to walk. Saint Nicholas is said to have begun his fasting while still on the breast, refusing to suckle except on Wednesdays and Fridays!

Joseph of Copertino

Joseph of Copertino was born of a poor family in Taranto in Italy at a time of religious oppression in the early seventeenth-century Reformation. Born in a stable, in his youth he appears to have been beset with disease and despair. He spent many years in sickness, though ultimately he was healed from an incurable disease by oil from the lamp of the Virgin of Calatone. He was believed to be somewhat simple-minded and gained the nickname of "gaping mouth" for behaving in a clumsy and imbecilic manner. It is said that he often erupted into sudden bursts of anger, and fell into long trances resulting in expressions of great love and piety.

He was eventually to become a priest but remained largely illiterate. He was continually subject to major bursts of miraculous and ecstatic behavior, far more dramatic in nature, according to his biographers, than that of any other saint in the whole of Christian history.

He made wine from water, created bread from nothing, drove out devils, healed, restored sight, commanded the weather, made prophetic statements with astonishing success, banished witchcraft and evil, and had an extraordinary affinity with animals and insects, particularly flies, who would take rest on his tongue or other parts of his face without his being evidently aware of their presence.

His practices were excessively ascetic: wherever he traveled he ate only roots and herbs and rarely changed his very basic hairshirt – though, by all accounts, he smelled always as sweet as flowers. He regularly flagellated himself and even punished bad thoughts by tearing flesh from his body with nails and pins.

What made Joseph of Copertino most famous were his extraordinary leaps through the air, which were accompanied by horrifying cries and shrieks. These "flights," as they were described by Prospero Lambertini (later to become Pope Benedict XV), the Devil's Advocate who undertook the examination of the application for his canonization, were numerous and prolonged and occurred while Joseph was in a state of ecstasy.

The flights ranged from early leaps of up to six or seven feet to much more astonishing and complex displays which carried the flying monk up into trees where he would appear to rest on branches that could never have sustained a man's weight. There he would perch for up to half an hour or more like a bird.

Another occasion gave witness to his lifting a massive, thirty-six-foot-high cross (after flying some seventy yards from the door of the friary) and placing it into the hole provided. According to depositions signed by those watching the event, ten men could not have lifted the cross.

Joseph went on to perform similar feats of unbelievable and miraculous "seizures" all over Italy in front of both the poor and gullible and the rich and sophisticated, with notable witnesses among the royalty of many lands.

More dramatic than any of the above miraculous deeds is the case of the flying monk. In his book The Hiding Places of God, John Cornwall introduces us to Joseph of Copertino, one of many saints who reputedly managed to elevate from the ground and actually fly without the aid of wings, motors, or any other mechanical device. There are said to have been at least fifty such individuals with this extraordinary capability, largely derived it seems from the ability to levitate.

In the Old Testament we find miracles sent directly from God, to guide His chosen people through the difficulties and perils they met when trying to fulfill His divine plan. Thus, for instance, God sends an angel who appears to Moses in the flames of a burning bush which is not consumed by the fire. God speaks from the bush and commands Moses to free the Hebrew tribes from Egyptian slavery. When Moses doubts his ability to achieve such a task, and wonders how the people will believe that he was chosen for it, God commands him to throw the rod in his hand to the ground. When Moses does so, the rod becomes a snake, and when God commands him to pick it up by its tail, the snake becomes again a rod. This miracle, God explains, will serve as proof to the Egyptian pharaoh that Moses has been sent by God on this mission.

Moses is again able to use his miraculous rod to part the waters of the sea when the Egyptian army is pursuing the fleeing Israelites. After they have crossed over by walking on dry land in the midst of the sea, he makes the waters close again, overwhelming the Egyptian army. Similarly, when the Israelites are crossing the desert in order to reach the Promised Land, they complain of hunger to Moses. God sends proof of His existence in the form of manna, the divine bread which will sustain them through their journey. When they complain of thirst, God tells Moses to strike a rock with his rod and water miraculously gushes forth from it so that the people may drink.

As we have seen from the first part of this book, the faithful in all quarters are subject to the enchantment of saints as workers of wonders and miracles. Strictly speaking, the Christian definition of miraculous powers is attributable solely to God's influence. A Christian saint does not perform the miracle personally, but as an instrument of the will of God. In Judaism, God chooses certain individuals as his instruments on earth and through them he performs miraculous deeds. Similar phenomena are recorded in other religions, although not as acts of God but as supernatural powers wielded by holy individuals. Within Buddhism for example, the supernatural powers that may occur within meditation or trance are not deemed truly miraculous, though in examining the Buddhist "iddhi" there is a close association.

Iddhi powers involve the adept in taking many different human forms, appearing, disappearing, and opening up the sky to reveal heaven. The meditator may also hear divine sounds, as well as sounds too far away to be heard by the normal ear, and be able to listen to other people's thoughts. The powers arise naturally when one has reached the deepest state of meditation, samadhi, in which the meditator passes through eight different levels of consciousness, higher than those normally experienced in everyday life. Buddhist teaching and practice states that at the fourth level of consciousness, the body becomes very light and malleable and the meditator is filled with a sense of bliss; this sensation is so extraordinary that it encourages the individual to go deeper into meditation and thus reach the other levels of consciousness. At the fourth level, however, the meditator acquires the power to recollect the past: not only are the events which have occurred in this life remembered, but also all the previous births, deaths, and lives, going far, far back beyond the individual past to the formation of the cosmos. Because of this power, the individual consciousness of the meditator merges with the consciousness of the universe so that all personal and cosmic events are amalgamated. This is why Buddhist Bodhisattvas and Arahants, those who have reached this level of

Opposite: *The Sai Baba ashram in India.* Left: *Sathya Sai Baba is known the world over for his miracles.*

consciousness, are considered greater than all the deities, for through their meditation they have spanned the gap between humanity and cosmic consciousness. From this state the meditator is able to tell the cycles that the cosmos undergoes and to foresee future cycles, and thus able to detect even the slightest fluctuation or movement of the universe.

A famous Arahant, Acharn Man, who lived in Thailand at the beginning of the century, is believed to have achieved these astounding powers. His biography was written by one of his disciples, who describes Acharn Man talking to the king of the gods, his retinue of deities and angels; his encounters with demons and wandering ghosts resulting in their conversion to Buddhism, and his exercise of the supernatural powers acquired through meditation. Acharn Man was also known for his skill in pacifying wild animals, such as fierce tigers, threatening elephants, screaming monkeys, and poisonous snakes, with his overwhelming cosmic love which he transmitted to the animals by speaking to them in a silent language. Despite the fact that Buddhist sacred texts tell of the supernatural powers that may be acquired in deep states of meditation, within the Buddhist tradition, and directly from Buddha's personal instruction, the adept is discouraged from becoming too deeply involved in the performance of the iddhi, as this is considered likely to prevent the rise to greater heights. The path towards the awakening of the individual might be lost through the seductions of the enjoyment of these extraordinary powers.

Within the Hindu tradition of magic and miracles there is a still more subtle viewpoint which is best exemplified by one particular Indian miracle-maker – Sathya Sai Baba. The glorious subcontinent of India is famous for the many individuals, gurus and masters of different religious definitions, who incarnate the saintly paradigm and bring light where there is darkness in the human heart. Sathya Sai Baba is one of these individuals, for he is revered as a saint in India. His deeds and inexplicable feats have made him well-known for his wonder-working powers. He is said to have begun manifesting miraculous powers very early in life, causing, for instance, his teacher's chair to be glued to his backside and performing other, pranksterish, miracles upon those around him.

The Wedding at Cana, during which Jesus miraculously transformed water into wine. By Duccio Buoninsegna, in the Museo dell'Opera del Duomo, Siena.

At the age of thirteen he fell into a seizure characterized by bouts of laughter, tears, song, and the recitation of holy scriptures, at the end of which he materialized sweets and flowers which he gave to his friends and neighbors.

His followers today regard him as the greatest living master, and the central feature of his teachings is his miracles. From a distance he may appear simply to be a fake, a magician without any greater depth than this, but if examined a little closer we find that the miraculous aspect of his teaching is much more than simple magic. He is said to cure illness and, following in the very best tradition of the miraculous, he has reputedly brought the dead back to life. He travels to distant areas without normal transport and can exist in more than one place at a time. He can perform surgical operations from a vast distance, and rather than changing water into wine, in a more practical vein he has been known to change water into gasoline.

The miracles that he is most famous for, however, are the occasions when he produces items out of thin air, such as books, sweets, pictures of himself, jewelry, watches, and numerous other items, apparently entirely at random. The most common material that appears in his miraculous hands is the sacred ash known as "vibhuti," of which he produces more than a pound each day. Ash is the most important holy symbol of the god Shiva, an emblem of ascetic concentration and of the power which is found in this state of deep meditation.

There are numerous houses dedicated to Sathya Sai Baba scattered around the world, functioning effectively as sub-centers of the cult, belonging to or occupied by devotees of the master. Within these houses, it is told, miracles also take place: pictures of the master produce ash in an inexplicable manner, objects appear and disappear, food is eaten by invisible spirits, drink appears from nowhere.

The central feature of these miraculous events, which at times resemble the effects of a poltergeist, seems to be that all the substances produced by the miracle-maker are intended to be given to the devotees. This is central to the Hindu ritual tradition of "prasad" (or food offering), in which items that have been in close contact with the master are given to disciples, rather in the same manner as relics of Christian saints produce cures for pilgrims. As such, the items materialized by Sathya Sai Baba transfer the efficacy of the master's power to the disciple.

The process of the miraculous as represented by Sathya Sai Baba might appear to be somewhat capricious, jarring perhaps with the inherent holiness traditionally associated with wonders of this type . And yet, in another sense, it conforms quite closely to other forms of miraculous behavior: Jesus, for instance, turned water into wine in order that his disciples might quench their thirst. The saintliness of this Indian guru, in the same way as the saintliness of the Christian holy man, therefore appears securely attached to the desire to do good to mankind, whatever particular format the miraculous behavior might take.

Below: *Pilgrims at Sarnath for the Dalai Lama.* Opposite: *The Pope prays at Fatima.*

PILGRIMAGES

Pilgrimages are a corollary of the human passion for holiness, and for experiencing the depths of mysteries we are not able to explain rationally. It is during a pilgrimage that the individual reaches aspects of the self and experiences events which are not otherwise accessible in ordinary human affairs. Pilgrimages are born out of the expectation of, the need for, and the desire to contact the divine dimension, and to be healed by this contact. Some sacred sites of devotion draw devotees who come together during a particular time of year, often astrologically determined, to celebrate a certain saint. Other pilgrimages are made by individuals who leave their familiar surroundings, suffer hardships along the way, and hope to find transcendence through visiting an extraordinary sequence of places and experiencing an extraordinary sequence of events. It is in these very particular spots on earth – our sacred places – that the possibility of a communion between the individual and a holy spirit gathers strength.

In Christianity we find a hierarchy in the holiness of pilgrimage sites. Jesus, as the founder of the religion, represents the uppermost pinnacle of sacredness, and thus all the locations where he lived and which he visited are considered sacred by all Christians. Jerusalem draws thousands of pilgrims every year, and the sacred shroud of Turin, allegedly the linen in which his body was wrapped after the crucifixion, and the only thing left in his sepulcher after his ascension, is the most powerful relic in Christendom.

The Blessed Virgin Mary, who comes next in the Christian holy hierarchy, has popularly been perceived as the mother of God and of all mankind.

She is believed to appear in moments of need and at times of darkness in order to bring a message of hope, encouraging all to follow the path of virtue. Marian shrines throughout the world are extremely powerful sites of pilgrimage. Possibly the most famous among these is the Shrine of Our Lady of Fatima, located in the plateau of Cova da Iria, near Leiria, in Portugal. Named after a twelfth-century Moorish princess, this

Below: *The sick visiting the sanctuary in Lourdes, hoping to be miraculously healed by its waters.* Opposite: *Bernadette Soubirous with Mother Alexandrine Roques, Superior of the Hospice at the time of the Marian apparitions in Lourdes.*

shrine was established after the Virgin Mary appeared to three peasant children on May 13, 1917, and on the same day of each subsequent month through October of the same year. The apparitions of the Virgin Mary were deemed miraculous by the local people, and by October 13, 1927, a huge crowd of 70,000 people had gathered on the site. On that day all witnessed a miraculous solar phenomenon after the Lady had appeared to the children. Thereafter, a chapel was built on the spot and named the Chapel of the Apparitions, where many miraculous healings have since occurred.

A similar shrine is dedicated to the Holy Blessed Mother in Lourdes, France. Here, in 1858, the eldest daughter of a poor miller, Bernadette Soubirous, had contact with a very beautiful lady, on eighteen occasions, in a shallow cave on the bank of the river

Gave. The lady pointed to a long-forgotten spring of water and encouraged Bernadette to pray and be penitent, and eventually revealed herself to be the Virgin Mary. Even though the visions took place when other people were present in the cave, no one but Bernadette could see or hear anything. The waters of this underground spring at Lourdes are famous for their miraculous properties, and thousands of people have been healed of incurable diseases at the shrine.

Marian apparitions are nearly always accompanied by an extraordinary miracle, as when the Lady appeared twice in 1531 to a native Mexican convert named Juan Diego, in Villa Guadalupe Hidalgo, now a northern neighborhood of Mexico City. In the first apparition, the Virgin commanded that a church be built in her honor. But because nobody would

believe Juan Diego she appeared a second time to give proof of her existence, which came in the form of an extraordinary painting portraying her image, now known as the Virgin of Guadalupe. Both the colors and the details of the painting are thought to have divine provenance. Here the Basilica of Our Lady of Guadalupe was built, and is today the chief religious center in Mexico.

In medieval times, pilgrims traveled great distances in order to renew their faith and purify their spirits. The most famous pilgrim route in Europe is that of Santiago of Compostela.

Santiago is the Spanish name for Saint James, whose shrine the city possesses. In 813 a tomb was discovered and it was supernaturally revealed that it contained the bones of the apostle Saint James the Great, who was martyred in Jerusalem in the year 44.

Legend tells that James had attempted to escape persecution and had landed on the shores of Spain. He had traveled inland and settled for a few years in the area which is now Santiago, converting the local population to the gospel of Jesus by performing miracles. He had then returned to the Holy Land where he was killed. His remains, however, were brought back to Spain for burial. A cathedral was eventually built on the spot by King Alfonso VI of Leon and Castile in 1078. Pilgrims claimed to receive visions and blessings when traveling on the great pilgrimage road that led to Santiago.

Even though Judaism rejects the idea of sainthood, the Holy Land of Israel has played an extremely significant role in the religion and continues to do so today. This is the land which was promised to Abraham, and to which the Hebrew

Opposite: *Pilgrims at the basilica of Our Lady of Guadalupe, Mexico City.*
Below: *A pilgrim embraces the statue of Our Lady, hoping to receive her grace.*

Below: *A view of Jerusalem showing the Western Wall on the Temple Mount (Mount Moriah), Judaism's holiest site; and above it, within the Haram al-Sharif (the Noble Sanctuary), the Dome of the Rock.* Opposite: *The Ka'bah sanctuary at Mecca, spiritual axis of the Muslim world.*

tribes who had fled Egypt traveled. Israel is, in many ways, synonymous with the earthly heaven in popular Jewish tradition.

Jerusalem, now the capital of Israel, is the main spiritual center of Jewish devotion. It is to this center that the Ark of the Covenant was moved by King David, after being held in several other sanctuaries. David wished to build a temple for the Ark on Mount Moriah, or the Temple Mount, where it was believed that Abraham had built the altar on which to sacrifice his son Isaac. In building the temple, David joined Israel's major religious site with the monarchy and the city itself into a central and unique symbol of the union of all the Israelite tribes.

The First Temple was, however, constructed by King David's son, Solomon in 957 BCE. It was an abode for the Ark and a place for assembly of all the people. The building faced eastward and consisted of three rooms: the porch, the Holy Place, and the Holy of Holies, where the Ark rested. This First Temple was destroyed by Nebuchadnezzar II of Babylon in 586 BCE, when the Ark was also lost. A second temple was then built after the exiled Hebrews returned from their Babylonian captivity in about 538 – 515 BCE, and it became again the center of religious life, housing the Holy Scriptures. This temple was rebuilt on a grand scale by Herod the Great, King of Judea (40 BCE - 4 CE), and was the focal point of the Jewish religion in the Roman world. Herod's temple was destroyed by the Romans in 70 CE after the Jewish Revolt. All that remains today is a portion of its Western Wall, popularly called the Wailing Wall by tourists. This is today a site of prayer and pilgrimage sacred to Jewish people, where

they lament the destruction of the Temple and pray for its restoration.

Mount Sinai is also considered an important site of pilgrimage, for it is here that God revealed the Ten Commandments to Moses.

The most sacred place for Muslims is the Ka'bah sanctuary at Mecca, in Saudi Arabia. Muhammad, the founder of Islam, was born here and it is towards Mecca that Muslims turn five times a day when praying. The pilgrimage to Mecca is one of the five fundamental pillars of Islam (the others being: the profession of faith, prayer, the payment of the zakat tax, and fasting during the month of Ramadan). All Muslims are required to undertake the pilgrimage to Mecca at least once in their lifetimes. The pilgrimage rite begins on the seventh and ends on the tenth day of the last month of the Muslim year. When the pilgrim is about six miles from the Holy City, he is required to wear two seamless garments and neither shaves nor cuts his hair or nails until the pilgrimage has ended. Once in Mecca, the pilgrims must walk seven times around the Ka'bah, kiss and touch the Black Stone housed in the sacred shrine, and ascend and run between Mount Safa and Mount Marwah seven times. The second stage of the pilgrimage consists of visiting Mina, a town a few miles away from Mecca, and Arafat, where all pilgrims must attend a sermon and spend an afternoon. The last rites consist of spending the night at Muzdalifah (between Arafat and Mina) and offering the sacrifice of the last day of the pilgrimage. According to Islamic tradition Abraham and Ishmael built the Ka'bah as the house of God.

Medina is the second most important site of pilgrimage for Islam, and is celebrated as the place from which Muhammad conquered the whole of Arabia after his flight from Mecca (622 CE). The Prophet's tomb is here, making Medina a sacred city, which only Muslims are permitted to enter.

The third sacred Muslim site is Jerusalem – also considered holy in Christianity and Judaism – where the Prophet Muhammad made his ascent to heaven and where God revealed to him the truth. The Dome of the Rock, in the Haram al-Sharif (on Mount Moriah) is the sacred shrine that draws many devoted pilgrims every year.

The ancient land of India is the birthplace of Hinduism; its sacred geography is honored by pilgrims who may find in this holy ground inspiration for emancipation. The land of India has become so deeply saturated in Hindu mythology and sacred scriptures, that everywhere there is a shrine or temple where travelers can nourish their spirits.

All over India, pilgrimages are taking place daily, on every scale, and in every region. It would be far too difficult to enumerate them all in this short section. The reasons for undertaking a holy journey are as many as the pilgrimages themselves. Benefits may be had from visiting specific places – temples or ponds dedicated to the Sun, for instance, are visited to recover from leprosy. Other places may be visited to ward off the dangers of adverse astrological aspects. Devotees can undertake a pilgrimage to gain worldly well-being (health, wealth, and children) or for a renewal of their faith and spirituality, to pray for rebirth in heaven or to take vows and become a wandering sannyasin.

When death is near, some devoted Hindus travel to the northern city of Varanasi (Benares) so as to die on the shores of the Ganges, the sacred river which will cleanse their souls of all sins. Brindavan, on the other hand, is the site of one of the main temples dedicated to the Lord Krishna, and hundreds of thousands of pilgrims go there every year to obtain darsan – the sight – and clarity of perception.

Because pilgrims are traveling all over India constantly, pilgrimage sites tend to be well organized, with priests attending to the needs of the devotees, and accommodation provided for the comfort of the visitors. Perhaps the greatest gatherings of all occur during the religious fairs – the "melas" – which may draw several million people at once in a celebration that occurs every twelve years in the cities of Allahabad, Hardwar, Ujjain, and Nasik. The four

main sites of Buddhist pilgrimage are connected with important events in the life of the Buddha: Lumbini was his birthplace; Bodh Gaya was where he became enlightened under the bodhi tree; Sarnath was the location of his first discourse as an enlightened being; and, finally, Kusinara is the place of his death (parinirvana). By far the most important site for Buddhists is Bodh Gaya, in central Bihar state in northern India. Here the Emperor Ashoka built a simple temple in the third century BCE to mark the spot where Prince Gautama Siddhartha attained enlightenment. This ancient building was replaced by the Mahabodhi temple which was erected in 1200 CE. Bodh Gaya is visited by thousands of pilgrims every year who seek the depth of meditation attained by the Buddha, and there renew their vow to undertake the inner journey towards awakening.

Opposite: *Ritual bathing in the Ganges on the ghats of Mizzarpur, north of Varanasi.*
Below: *The Buddha by the bodhi tree, a temple carving in Java.*

Saint Candida's shrine in Dorset, England.

EPILOGUE

Saints, as we have seen in the brief journey through the different paths of sainthood undertaken in this book, represent an exalted state of humanity; a strong paradigm which forces an expansion of consciousness upon us. Saints have, throughout all ages and cultures, always been uniquely important – as well as providing aid, fellowship, and example, they incarnate for the ordinary human being that "otherness" which brings wholesome meaning to life. And yet, despite the fact that saints are the products of the human need to feel and live the religious life, there is a very notable absence of vital ideals of sanctity in modern secular cultures.

Our age and society is characterized by the eclipse of the sacred – mankind seems no longer to need or crave religiousness in everyday life. Perhaps this is because the dominant ideals and aspirations today are an expression of consumerism and individuality. The bourgeois lifestyle supposedly fulfills us, so much so that we no longer wonder about the mysteries woven within our existence. We find modern saints in the "less developed" areas, such as India and the far East in general, or among the so-judged "superstitious" Catholic countries. But is it really true that we no longer experience the need to fulfill our souls? The emerging New Age movements and the impact they have upon the popular imagination might be underscoring the hunger for "spiritual," and not material, nourishment.

What is the fulfillment provided by saints? Firstly, their very existence validates the feeling in each individual that life is wider and deeper than it

A Hindu temple in Panchgani, India.

appears in the light of our small everyday struggles. Secondly, the acts of believing, visiting, and seeing saints bring humanity together in humility – when in the presence of a saint we experience a sense of community and a communal bond between the divinity and humanity. Thirdly, and perhaps as a consequence of the first two effects, we might feel a sense of elation and luminous joy, because the normal boundaries we perceive as enclosing human life are stretched. The ego-self melts down, and embraces the spiritual dimension. And lastly, our attention shifts from the small to the grand in the presence of a saint – we find ourselves more ready to say "yes" to the fullness of existence in a religious context, rather than the perpetual "no" which often seems to be our sole motto in everyday life.

Saints are admittedly ambiguous figures; they are like us, and yet qualitatively different from us. As such, they point the way towards our own potential inner fulfillment. They offer proof that we acquire authentic selves in the measure that we acquire God and the divine – and they provide us with a "living" example of that measure. By loving God and by following the paths of sainthood, we become the goal and the result of that love. And in that path we become healed and transformed by discovering the deepest meaning and true face of the mystery of existence. Whether we embrace the saint as a teacher or as a miracle-worker, as an exemplar of the ultimate virtue or as an intercessor, or simply as a "chosen one" who has a special relation to the divine, the saint is there to remind us that true fulfillment comes only when we are able to embrace the higher dimension within ourselves.

The Assumption of the Virgin. Alterpiece ascribed to Francesco Botticini.

dictione diabolicaru artui.

x   Q°d de ineffabili gra sua. corde & ore
ds inceffabilit laudandus e.

xi   Q°d simphonia iununanimitate & con
cordia pferenda e.

xii   Q°d uerbum corp° symphonia aute
spm. & armonia diuinitate uerbu
u humanitate filiu designat.

xiii   Q°d p symphonia racionaliutaru tor
peni anima excitat ad uigilandu.

xiiii   Q°d symphonia dura corda emollit.
& humore 9punctionis inducit. &
spm scm aduocat.

xv   Q°d fidelis omi deuotione icessant
uibilare debet.

xvi   Verba dauid de eadem re.

B I B L I O G R A P H Y

Ahir, B.R. Buddhist Shrines in India. Dehli, B.R. Publishing Corporation, 1986.

Al-Ghazali, Muhammad. Remembrance and Prayer – The Way of the Prophet Muhammad. London, The Islamic Foundation, 1986.

Attar, Farid al-Din. Muslim Saints and Mystics. London, Penguin Books, 1990.

Attwater, Donald, The Penguin Dictionary of Saints. London, Penguin Books, 1983.

Bender, Hans. La Realta Nascosta — Precognizioni, Sogni, Veggenze, Profezie, Il Miracolo del Sangue di San Gennaro. Roma, Edizioni Mediterranee, 1990.

Bockenham, Osbern. A Legend of Holy Women. Notre Dame, University of Notre Dame Press, 1992.

Chenu, Bruno and Claude Prud'homme, France Quere, Jean-Claude Thomas. The Book of Christian Martyrs. London, SCM Press, 1990.

Coppleston, F.C. Aquinas – An Introduction to the Life and Work of the Great Medieval Thinker. London, Penguin Books, 1955.

Dundas, Paul. The Jains. London and New York, Routledge, Chapman, and Hall, 1992.

Harris, Lis. Holy Days – The World of a Hasidic Family. New York, Summit Books, 1985.

Hawley, John Stratton, ed. Saints and Virtues. Berkeley, London, University of California Press, 1987.

Hawley, John Stratton and Mark Juergensmayer. Songs of the Saints of India. New York and Oxford, Oxford University Press, 1988.

Hinnels, John R., ed. A Handbook of Living Religions. London, Penguin Books, 1991.

Ishigami, Zenno, ed. Disciples of the Buddha. Tokyo, Kosei Publishing Co., 1989.

Kieckhefer, Richard and George D. Bond, ed. Sainthood – Its Manifestations in World Religions. Berkeley, London, University of California Press, 1988.

Marshall, Michael. Saints Alive! Biblical Reflections on the Lives of the Saints. London, SPCK, 1992.

Pusey, Edward Bouverie, trans. The Confessions of Saint Augustine. New York, Quality Paperback Bookclub, 1991.

Rappel. Los Santos que nos Ayudan. Madrid, Ediciones Temas de Hoy, 1992.

Taylor, John W. The Coming of the Saints – Imaginations and Studies in Early Church History and Tradition. Thousand Oaks, Artisan sales, 1985.

Thomas, Keith. Religion and the Decline of Magic. London, Penguin Books, 1971.

Wiesel, Elie. Souls On Fire – Portraits and Legends of Hasidic Masters. London, Weidenfeld and Nicholson, 1972.

Woodward, Kenneth L. Making Saints – Inside the Vatican: Who Become Saints, Who Do Not, And Why. London, Chatto & Windus, 1991.

A C K N O W L E D G M E N T S

National Gallery, London: 6, 88 (bottom), 170, 193, 195, 246. Fernando Lauand: 8, 38, 39, 43 (left), 72, 111, 205, 237. Mike Shoring: 9, 10, 109, 128/129, 232. Ghandi Foundation: 11. Osho International Foundation: 12, 13. Scala, Firenze: 14, 21, 27, 35, 37, 38/39, 40, 41, 49, 52, 60, 65, 67, 68, 78, 92, 139, 146, 147, 153, 154,173, 177, 179, 182, 183, 186, 190, 198, 200, 203, 222, 227, 230, 247, 254. Hodalic Arne: 15, 23, 30/31, 47, 54, 70, 127, 128 (left), 130, 131, 145, 148, 156, 162, 207, 219, 242. Bodleian Library, Oxford: 17, 28, 42, 75, 97, 98, 102 (both), 104, 105, 107, 110, 121 (bottom), 174, 197, 223(right), 224. Derik Gardiner: 18 (bottom), 29, 149 (top), 157, 159, 160/161, 209, 210/211, 212, 213, 243. Adina Ansel: 18 (top). Gianluca DeSantis: 19, 122, 132 (bottom), 134/135, 152, 158, 167, 215, 217, 240 (right), 241. Abbey of St.Hildegard: 24, 34, 251. Jean Williamson/Mick Sharp: 26. Mick Sharp: 33,36, 43 (right), 56, 57 (both), 58/59, 66, 99, 168, 214, 220, 244. Ripon Cathedral: 37. St.Chad's Cathedral: 44. Ancient Art & Architecture, London: 45, 117, 119, 185, 188, 189. Westminster Abbey: 50, 51. St.Peter's Church, Ireland: 55. Victoria & Albert Museum, London: 74, 123. Julliet Soester: 76, 79 (left), 90, 91, 96, 103, 238. Bridgeman Art Library, London, {Museo Da Pesaro, Venice 77; Gemaldegalerie, Kassel 83; Galleria degli Uffizi, Florence 84; British Library, London 86; Museo del Prado, Madrid 90 (top); Bury Art Gallery, Lanceshire 94; Museum of the History of Religion, St.Petersburg 95}. Judah L. Magnus Museum, Berkeley: 80. Lubavitch Foundation, Vishinsky: 81. Jewish Museum, London: 82, 87. British Library: 112, 113, 180. Colorific, London: 114. Peter Sanders: 116, 239. International Rumi Committee: 118. Premgit: 120, 121 (top), 124, 125, 126, 132 (top), 133, 150 (top), 151, 160 (left), 165, 240 (left), 245. Barnaby's Picture Library, London: 142, 143. Art Screen Prints: 144, 150 (bottom). Carol Neiman: 155. National Palace Museum, Taiwan: 161 (right), 164. Tibet Foundation: 166. Labyrinth collection: 163. Bruno Kortenhorst: 181. St.Joan's Alliance, Liverpool: 196. Bord Failte Photo: 216, 225. Canterbury Cathedral: 221. Dhiresha: 223 (left). Monastery Pius XII, Fatima: 233. Catholic Association Pilgrimage Trust: 234. Maison-Mere des Soeurs de la Charite de Nevers: 235. Mexicolore, Sean Sprague: 236.

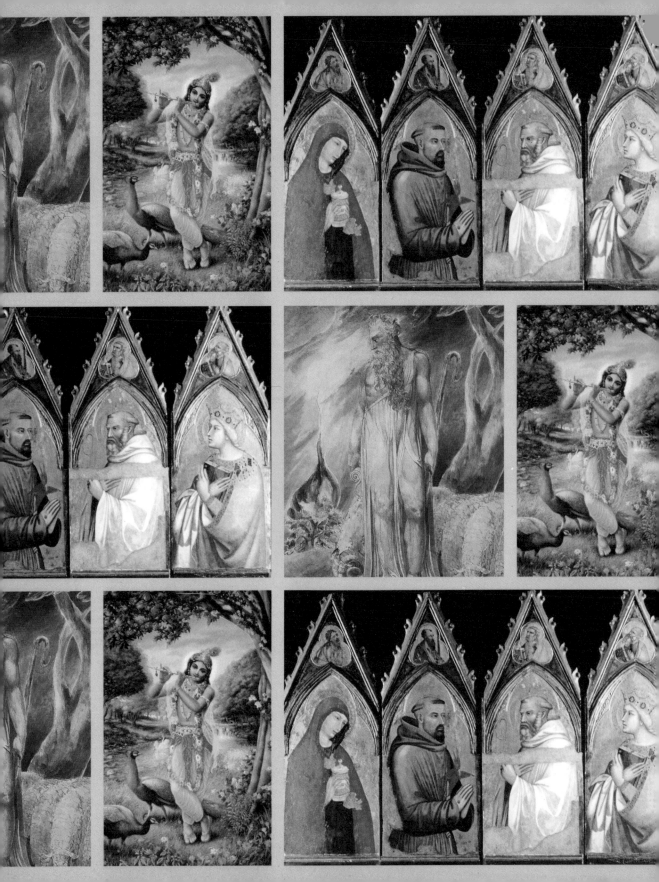